# Making Impossibilities

# POSSIBLE

## by
## Dr. Maureen Anderson

### edited by
### Julie Riggs

Winword
publishing house
Phoenix, Arizor

D0954191

FIRST EDITION

Published by **Winword Publishing, Inc.**
3520 E. Brown Road
Mesa, AZ 85213

480-985-6156
www.winwordpublishing.com

ISBN 1-58588-129-5

*Making Impossibilities Possible*

# Table of Contents

# Introduction

Winston Churchill believed that he was "born for such a time as this." With that belief, he led Britain to victory over Hitler's Germany and became one of the greatest leaders of all time. He was not the only one born for such a time, however. Every person ever born was intended for such a time as this. God created you with a destiny and a purpose and it is no accident that you were born when you were. The problem for most people is that they fail to recognize how important they are and they give up on their dreams long before they are fulfilled.

This book was written in an attempt to bridge the gap between where you are and where God has destined you to be. Step by step, chapter by chapter, it will help you piece together the principles of God, that lead to "the abundant life." With the information in this book, you can build a picture of God's destiny for you and plant it in your heart. Then you can go on to create that destiny in your life.

As you journey through this book, you will learn God's ideas in an organized, coherent manner which will enable you to achieve the results you have desired since you were first born again. The real joy in life comes from persevering in Christ to the finish line. The greatest joy is attained when you receive the promises that Christ has purchased for you. Moreover, if the truth was made known to you, you would realize that God has already given you the ability through His Word to achieve success in your life and be more than a winner in Him.

I have personally put every one of the principles in this book to the test over the past thirty years. Therefore, I can tell you from first-hand experience, the results have been beyond what I would ever hope or dream. Know that God is calling you to success and know that in Christ you already have it. No amount of learning will ever give you the success you desire in Christ. It is only the understanding by the Holy Spirit and application of right thinking and speaking that counts. Regardless of what I or anyone else might say, you are going to have to prove these principles work for yourself by doing them. You can journey from where you are now to a greater awareness of Christ—of God's dream for you—and your true abilities in Christ.

Like Churchill, you must also believe that you were born for such a time as this to bring God's truth into victory in both your life and your children's lives. The cries go out from the heavenly Father to bring forth His Word by the anointing to its victory. Releasing the anointing and coming into covenant agreement with God's Word will empower you to rise up and fulfill your personal destiny. I urge you to join me on this journey to success in Christ.

# 1
## *Making Impossibilities Possible*

Nothing on earth seemed to exceed the heat of June that summer in Arizona—nothing except the pain that attacked my body. My legs, arms and joints would hardly move. Some mornings the pain was so severe that my husband Tom had to help me out of bed. It was a very frightening time, to say the least. The doctor's report said rheumatoid arthritis. "You'll be in a wheelchair within two weeks, and you won't be able to get out of bed before Christmas."

As soon as we arrived home from the doctor, Tom and I came into agreement in prayer that the disease would leave me as quickly as the enemy had put it on me. I believed at that very moment that I was already healed. I received a "seed" of God that implanted healing in my heart. I connected spiritually to the Holy Spirit, who led me every day to the Word of God. He renewed my mind and brought back to my soul the remembrance of healing.

During that time, I chose to see myself running, leaping, bicycling, and doing athletic activities that I previously had no interest in. Within two months, as quickly as the disease had come, it left me. Today, I am a skier and a runner. I enjoy physical activities at last.

In my own power, I could not have changed myself one bit, but God did not intend for me to live in sickness or failure. Instead, He gave me the key to making effective, permanent, God-inspired changes in my life through the practical application of the Gospel—the death, burial, and resurrection of Christ (1 Corinthians 15:1, 3-4). God did more than I asked for when His healing became visible. I want to share with you what I have learned these past thirty years, in addition to what God revealed to me in those two months. He not only brought about awesome healing, but also tremendous increase in every area of my life. God does not intend for any of us to be satisfied with lack in our lives.

## 2
### Have God-Like Faith

When we grow up with lack in our lives, those images keep us in poverty, sickness and defeat until we are set free from them. If we were raised in severe poverty, we heard lack all the time: "We can't buy that." "We can't do that." "We don't have this." "Hope we can pay the bills."

Because of these hopeless confessions, people often develop an image of lack within their subconscious. When words go forth, there are pictures painted in the mind to match those words. Not only are pictures implanted, but also behavior is embedded to accompany the image of lack.

Similarly, when we come into agreement with lack in our souls, we receive lack as a reward. From that unfaithful time to now, it has had dominion in our lives.

Then we become Christians and we hear of the blessings. We hear that all the promises are assured to us in Christ. But what is really ruling in us is the image that's been planted in our hearts that we've agreed with in the past. Such an image constantly causes us to repeat our family's history of illness, poverty, divorce—any lack of abundance of

God's blessings. Do you know that you repeat history unless Jesus comes in and sets you free? You can't change yourself, but Jesus did. He changed you from that power of lack in your life to the power of abundance by His works.

I remember when the Holy Spirit first showed Tom and me that God wanted us to prosper, and that for the sake of the kingdom of God, we were to seek His prosperity. I thought to myself, "It will be a miracle for my husband to come into prosperity. After all, he was raised with extreme lack in his life and poverty in his home."

Tom told me later what he did to respond to that calling in our lives. He told me that even though the enemy will throw everything he can at us to discourage us and make us quit, we're not quitters. We've already won in Christ.

He also told me how he dealt with that lack in his life. He said he called every thought or action that was contrary to God's Word and purposes "sin." He then saw the sin nailed to the cross, because Jesus became sin for us on the cross. In this way, Tom kept breaking poverty's power, its image and its life, until I found him easily agreeing with the abundance of God. The change in him was miraculous.

Sometimes it takes a little piece at a time to break a lifestyle that has been planted in us. The Old Testament tells us that bit by bit, we take the land until we're strong enough to possess it and keep it.

Therefore, we don't get discouraged. Instead, we receive the prosperity of the Lord. We need to keep this in mind to break all those thought patterns, images, and behavior patterns in our lives. God will change us and change us so that we can flow in Him and not be condemned.

> He called every thought or action that was contrary to God's Word and purposes "sin."

In the following verse, God is saying He wants us to take possession of His promises by driving out the thoughts and attitudes that oppose those promises.

> *Drive out all the inhabitants of the land before you. Destroy all their carved images and their cast idols, and demolish all their high places. Take possession of the land and settle in it, for I have given you the land to possess.* (Numbers 33:52-53)

When we drive out the lack, He will change us so that we can flow in Him. If we have abundance in our hearts and we see that we have the blessing, then we'll keep getting more and we'll continue to have abundance.

> *Whoever has will be given more; whoever does not have, even what he has will be taken from him.* (Mark 4:25)

The rich get richer because they have an image of themselves as wealthy. It's an image of wealth within them. They have an image of the abundance. In that image they keep sowing seed, and seed produces after its kind. This imagery is a principle of sowing and reaping.

A person who has lack within and sees his life ruled by poverty or deficiency will have even what little he possesses taken from him. Although it may not seem fair, this person is sowing seeds of lack—actions, thoughts, and mannerisms—that push abundance away. This person will harvest the lack because every seed produces according to its kind. The enemy wants to keep us in lack because he knows that such lack will expand until we have nothing.

People say that the poor get poorer. People who are raised in poverty or oppression will stay there the rest of their lives. In addition, their children will remain in that framework.

We, however, do not have to remain in lack because we are heirs of God's promises together with Christ. When we are born again, we become children of God.

*Now if we are children, then we are heirs—heirs of God and coheirs with Christ, if indeed we share in his sufferings in order that we may also share in his glory.* (Romans 8:17)

The previous chapter discusses death on the cross as a daily experience for the Christian. In Numbers 21:8-9, God told the people to look at the bronze snake on the pole, and then they would be healed and the power of that curse would be broken.

We see that Jesus took our lack upon Him when He was nailed to the cross in our place. He broke the power of the curse because He wants us to prosper. The Bible says He delights in our prosperity. His Word says He has abundance for us.

**God Has Abundance for Us**

*The LORD will open the heavens, the storehouse of his bounty, to send rain on your land in season and to bless all the work of your hands. You will lend to many nations but will borrow from none.* (Deuteronomy 28:12)

Giving to nations sounds like abundance! God wants us to come into agreement with what He says in his Word. What his Word says is sometimes overwhelming to us, but when we agree with it, we know that God has the power to do what He says.

*They feast on the abundance of your house;*
*    you give them drink from your river of de-*
*    lights.*
(Psalm 36:8)

We feast on the abundance God has provided for us.

*In times of disaster, they will not wither;*
*in days of famine, they will enjoy plenty.*
(Psalms 37:19)

*They will come and shout for joy on the heights*
*of Zion;*
*they will rejoice in the bounty of the*
*LORD—*
*the grain, the new wine and the oil,*
*the young of the flocks and herds.*
*They will be like a well-watered garden,*
*and they will sorrow no more.*
(Jeremiah 31:12)

*"I will satisfy the priests with abundance,*
*and my people will be filled with my*
*bounty"*
*declares the LORD.*
(Jeremiah 31:14)

*You will have plenty to eat, until you are full,*
*and you will praise the name of the LORD*
*your God,*
*who has worked wonders for you;*
*never again will my people be shamed.*
(Joel 2:26)

In Isaiah 61:7, the Lord tells us we will get a double portion. The New Covenant is a double portion right now of all that we heard from the Old Covenant or the Old Testament. God wants us to come into agreement with His Word. If our experiences do not match with what God says, then we need to change our experiences. We have the power to do that by seeing our experiences as God reveals them to us. God's Word is our standard, and if we do not match up to it, then we need to change ourselves, not the Word of God.

> If we are children, then we are heirs.

As the Word says, if we are children, then we are heirs. To be an heir of someone, that person must first die. Suppose that somebody you loved owned the whole world, including all the love, peace, joy, goodness, wealth and health in the universe. Suppose that person died, and you were asked to come to a reading of the will. There you sit listening to the lawyer telling you that all the inheritance is left to you. You get the whole inheritance; the Word of God is opened up, and it tells us that Jesus died and we get it all.

Unfortunately, many times we go home and forget that the will has been read. We forget the inheritance, and we often do not receive what is rightfully ours. Sadly, we do not apply what we inherited to expand the kingdom of God. After all, that is the purpose of the inheritance—sharing God's kingdom with the rest of the world. All that love, joy, and wealth is given to us to help spread the good news of Jesus. It is our heart's desire to see the Word of God go forth, because of the love of Christ that is in us.

### Imitate God's Faith

We need to attack our lack for the expansion of the kingdom of God worldwide. You have to have God-like faith to attack your lack. The Bible tells us to imitate God's faith.

> *"Have faith in God," Jesus answered. "I tell you the truth, if anyone says to this mountain, 'Go, throw yourself into the sea,' and does not doubt in his heart but believes that what he says will happen, it will be done for him. Therefore I tell you, whatever you ask for in prayer, believe that you have received it, and it will be yours." (Mark 11:22-24)*

Therefore, to have God-like faith, we say to that mountain of lack in our lives, "Lack, be gone. Be cast into the sea." If we do not doubt in our hearts, but believe what we have said, it will be done for us.

Lack does not necessarily mean poverty. It can be your marriage that is not a kingdom marriage, a friendship that has turned sour, depression or perhaps even sickness. The Bible instructs us to cleanse our house from those things that are not according to God's Word.

We do this by imitating God's faith. First, God thinks abundance in whatever He is creating. We need to get used to God's thoughts and to His way of thinking. Our thoughts and our ways are created within our boundaries and limitations. These limitations come from deep within us. As a result, we can only have faith for certain things. When we take these limited thoughts to God and pray them, we have it all backwards. Our thoughts do not need faith because we already know what we can accomplish. When we pray in our own thoughts, we are in control and know we cannot fail. We need to think God's thoughts.

> *"For my thoughts are not your thoughts,*
> *neither are your ways my ways,"*
> *declares the* LORD.
> *"As the heavens are higher than the earth,*
> *so are my ways higher than your ways*
> *and my thoughts than your thoughts."*
> (Isaiah 55:8-9)

Even though we may confess God's Word over our situation, we still limit ourselves because of our thinking. On the other hand, when we receive God's thoughts, we lay down our own control and receive His power for the situation. He matches His thoughts with where He lives and with His standards.

We asked God what His thoughts were for our church, and He told us He would not limit the work. The only limits we would have were the ones we placed on it ourselves. When we received God's Word for this church, and He said that our church would lend to nations, I figured I better come into agreement with God. As I received His thoughts and His visions, I understood that we were to bring people out of poverty and oppression throughout the world. At the same time I received these words, there was also the fear that I could not accomplish the awesome task that God had set before me.

This overwhelming fear of failure often happens when we receive an awesome appointment from God. At that point, we have to die to ourselves. Just like Abraham, we have to face the fact that we cannot do it in and of ourselves.

### Receive God's Power

In God's vision and dream, we cannot do what He asks us to do, but He has already done it! We have to receive from Him the power to accomplish our destiny, and we have to be fully persuaded that He has done it all. We receive it as having all been done based on Him. As we receive His visions and dreams, we also need to know that everything He asks of us, He has already made more than the complete provision for.

God thinks thoughts toward you. He has already thought your abundance, and He wants you to receive what He thinks.

> *"For I know the plans [thoughts] I have for you," declares the LORD, "plans to prosper you and not to harm you, plans to give you hope and a future."* (Jeremiah 29:11)

After thinking, God sees what is not seen. He has a vision. In the King James Version, Proverbs 29:18 tells us that without a vision, the people perish. God is a God of vision. He saw the universe before He created it. He wants to give us his vision so we do not perish, falter, or fail.

> *By faith we understand that the universe was formed at God's command, so that what is seen was not made out of what was visible.* (Hebrews 11:3)

The Bible tells us that Jesus is the express image of the invisible God. The Word of God reveals God, making Him visible to us. Therefore, what was not visible became visible through God speaking the Word. Thus, what is hidden to us becomes visible as we speak the Word.

After seeing His thoughts, God speaks His thoughts. God calls things into being.

*...the God who gives life to the dead and
calls things that are not as though they were.*
(Romans 4:17b)

One night while fellowshipping with Oral Roberts and his wife, Oral shared with us that he once had an appendicitis attack. Even before he went to the doctor, he and his wife agreed together in prayer that no surgeon would cut on him, and that he would receive the healing that Jesus bought for him. What I thought was most impressive is that they ended their prayer looking each other in the eye and saying, "And we will not break agreement."

To finish the story, Oral Roberts was examined and the first X-rays revealed a huge vibrating appendix that appeared ready to burst. As he was looking at the infected appendix on the screen, a warmth came over him, and he watched his appendix return to normal. He went home with his wife without having surgery, because they had agreed verbally that no surgeon was going to cut on his appendix. Oral Roberts said that he had "called in his receipt" to receive his rightful inheritance.

*As the rain and the snow
    come down from heaven,
and do not return to it
    without watering the earth
and making it bud and flourish...*

*so is my word that goes out from my mouth:*
  *It will not return to me empty,*
*but will accomplish what I desire*
    *and achieve the purpose for which I sent*
    *it.*

(Isaiah 55:10-11)

So, we see in both the life of Oral Roberts and in the Scripture that speaking the Word produces abundance. Rain comes, the grass grows green, and we reap the benefits. Filled with power, the Word accomplishes the vision, dream, and purpose of God.

Once our son, Jason, and his wife, Kelli, were sharing with us their desire to sell their car. Time had gone by without the car selling. After I shared with them about Oral Roberts, they went home and came into agreement in prayer. Within half an hour, the car was sold! When God's Word is received, His Word of promise will never be barren.

When you receive His Word, speak it, hear it, write it down. God writes His Word; He writes it on our hearts, He has written the Bible, and He commands us to write it down.

*Write down the revelation*
  *and make it plain on tablets*
  *so that a herald may run with it.*

(Habakkuk 2:2)

Write down the Word that is given to you that you have been speaking and that you have come into agreement with, for behind that Word is a vision.

*He who was seated on the throne said, "I am making everything new!" Then he said, "Write this down, for these words are trustworthy and true." (Revelation 21:5)*

Have you ever noticed that when you take all the thoughts that the Lord has placed in your mind and try to remember them all, that you just wear your brain out? But, when you write them down, you know they are done. God does it. He accomplishes His purpose.

God is a God of structure and order, so it makes sense to write things down. God is a doer. He makes things happen. If your experience is that you hear the Word but do not do the Word, then you need to receive His plan and go do it. You need to stop living by your own experiences and start living by the Word of God. A person who hears the Word and does it is like the man who built his house with a solid foundation. He will have a house built on the Rock.

## Build a Blessing Consciousness

How do we go about building a blessing consciousness and the God-like faith of abundance? We do it God's way and we think abundance. We must stop thinking the way the devil thinks about us and take on God's thoughts of us. We see the vision, say it, write it down, and now we think God-thoughts. We see ourselves with the mind's "eye of faith," already possessing God's desire of abundant life and success, which is God's inheritance for us.

> When we visualize what the Word says, we bring the subconscious into agreement.

The subconscious mind of the soul cannot distinguish between actual possession of abundance and the mere confessing of it. This is a truth, a law governing the way God created humans. Whatever the image in the subconscious mind is, the person will adhere to it in life. That image will govern the attitude and lifestyle of the individual. Accordingly, when we visualize what the Word says, we bring the subconscious into agreement, because the subconscious actually thinks we have it now.

The enemy, however, has taken this key to visualizing and counterfeited it. To withstand this type of attack, we must counterattack our lack through agreeing with the Word and seeing the power of God for the vision He has given us.

Learning to speak the Word aloud is a vital aspect of agreeing with the Word and developing God's vision in the mind.

*The tongue has the power of life and death,*
*and those who love it will eat its fruit.*
(Proverbs 18:21)

Soon we become comfortable with the idea of abundant success and becoming co-heirs with Christ. At first, it seems awkward to receive such overwhelming blessings. But, the awkwardness of the flesh hanging on to its vision of poverty, divorce, and disease has to go!

The result of receiving God's blessings is that we can give on all occasions. Then wealth is attracted to us like a magnet to metal. When we succeed in convincing our subconscious mind to come into agreement with the Word by speaking it aloud, the mustard seed faith begins.

Our subconscious mind will automatically seek ways of making us feel the reality of this before it is visible to the natural eye. Our spirit and soul are then in agreement with each other, because our subconscious is in agreement with the Word of God. Our spirit was in agreement with the Word when we became Christians, but the conflict within us is seated in a subconscious soul that wars against God's Word. The subconscious causes turmoil in the Christian, but when it comes into agreement with God's Word, the soul comes into submission to the spirit man, and there is power to perform the believing.

*Now to him who is able to do immeasurably more than all we ask or imagine, according to his power that is at work within us...* (Ephesians 3:20)

If we want to be receivers of God's promise of increase, blessings, and success, we must never worry about whether or not we will receive what we desire. Job made the remark that "what I feared has come upon me" (Job 3:25). If we insist upon constantly worrying about not having money, or fearing that we will lose what we do have, we are absolutely guaranteed to have the same testimony as Job. We attract into our lives the very things we do not want through worry and fear. Worry about failure is extremely counterproductive.

# 3
## God Ordained You to Live in Abundance

We want to be flooded with life, to know God, to know who we are, and to know the hope of our calling, the glorious riches of our inheritance in the saints, and the incomparably great power for those who believe. Therefore, we must surrender to the will of God so we can enter into the abundance He has ordained in our lives, and so that we might know abundance through spiritual wisdom and spiritual understanding. Through this abundance, we will know we can be fruitful in every good work and be strengthened with all power according to His glorious might.

As believers, we come into covenant agreement with the Word of God. We do this as though we were signing a contract or covenant. We draw on the faith that has already been placed within us, so the message of the Word of God is mixed with faith to benefit us.

In the last chapter, we focused on Jesus' statement in Matthew 13:12:

*Whoever has will be given more, and he will have an abundance. Whoever does not have, even what he has will be taken from him.* (Matthew 13:12)

This Scripture refers to agreement. If we come into agreement with abundance, and if we think abundance, speak abundance, and see abundance, then we are in agreement with the kingdom of God. God has brought us into His kingdom through being born again. Jesus, speaking in John 10:10, emphasizes this point:

> *I have come that they may have life, and have it to the full.* (John 10:10b)

The life He speaks of is the true life of God. All that God has and all that God is, He gives to us.

We are heirs of God and joint heirs with Jesus Christ. When we come into the truth of our inheritance, we have to leave the examples of significant authority figures and the falsehoods that we have been taught all through our lives by our experiences. We leave all that, because our testimony has to line up with the Word of God. God's Word is the truth, and if the words of our mouths fail to match it, then we need to get rid of the false testimony.

Choosing to live in the abundance of God, thinking God-like thoughts, and talking God-like talk, will produce after its own kind, and abundance will take us over as a result. God does not know lack; He only knows abundance. Therefore, as we sow abundance in our thought-lives and in our mouths, we reap abundance.

In a wheat field, one seed produces a stalk with thirty, sixty, or a hundred seeds on it. We can sow those thirty, sixty, or hundred seeds to produce that many more plants. You see that if you sow seed to produce a plant with one hundred seeds, and then replant those hundred seeds, your harvest will contain 10,000 seeds. That is a total of 10,100 seeds that developed from one seed.

> God does not know lack; He only knows abundance.

God's Word is like that seed. We reap whatever we sow in our thoughts, lives and conversation. The seed produces after its kind. When we sow the abundance spoken of in God's Word, we get more and more abundance in our lives.

You may say, "Wait a minute. The Bible says that the love of money is the root of all evil."

I'm not speaking of money here. I'm talking about abundance in every area of your life—marriage, children, ministry, health—anything that affects your quality of life. There is a difference between loving money, which is greed, and loving the abundance of God, which is receiving his benefits for the purpose of spreading his Word.

**We Receive So We Can Give**

> *For the sake of the house of the LORD our God,*
> *I will seek your prosperity.*
>                                    (Psalm 122:9)

God wants us to have abundance of wealth in the house of the Lord, so that the ministry can go forth. He needs us to prosper in order to cover the earth with the gospel and minister to the nations. We do not receive a blessing so that we can take it in for ourselves; the Word says we are to give it to someone else. As we receive, we give, and then we receive and give again. This is not the love of money; it is the love of God with all our substance.

God has streets of gold. He has houses built of jasper, emeralds, diamonds, and pearls. Yet, there is no evil in God, and we are to be like-minded.

When we receive the prosperity that is in the Word, it produces after its kind. This prosperity is righteous, holy, and godly unto the Lord, and it will drive greed out of your life!

God is faithful and His Word is useful to instruct us in righteousness, to train us, and to correct us. We don't have to be afraid of the prosperity of the Lord, because the prosperity of the Lord will deal with the things within us that are contrary to God. As we meditate and give ourselves to the Word, whatever is in our lives that is not of God will be revealed to us by the Holy Spirit. We can choose either life or death; we can choose to go God's way, or we can choose to be in agreement with the sin in our lives and to let that sin be destructive.

*Do not be deceived: God cannot be mocked. A*
*man reaps what he sows. The one who sows to*
*please his sinful nature, from that nature will*
*reap destruction; the one who sows to please the*
*Spirit, from the Spirit will reap eternal life.*
(Galatians 6:7- 8)

Just ignoring prosperity out of fear that you
might have greed in your life does not guarantee that
greed is not already operating in your life. This attitude is simply denial of reality. People can be poor
and still be full of greed and the love of money. Since
lack is not in the kingdom of
God, people with lack usually have greed in their lives.
Greed takes in and does not
give out. The greedy person
does not sow seed, and usually finds himself in a place

He needs us to prosper in
order to cover the
earth with the gospel and
minister to the nations.

where he has no seed to sow. Even when he finds a
seed to sow, he's in fear and holds onto it. Greed is
afraid of losing its seed.

Wealthy people also live as though they have
nothing, because greed holds their wealth. They do
not enjoy living, because they cannot give and bless
the kingdom of God. Remember, Jesus says that
the person who does not have will lose even the little
he does have. By this He is saying that the person
who believes in lack will produce seed of that kind,

reaping little or nothing, and the lack will get worse and worse.

We are in a land flowing with milk and honey. When God speaks of milk and honey in the Old Testament, He is saying He will take the Israelites out of bondage in Egypt and to the Promised Land. This is a picture of being born again and of coming into the kingdom of God.

God has rescued us from a kingdom of darkness, and brought us into the kingdom of his dear son (Colossians 1:13). "Milk and honey" refers to the very richest, the very best, the most abundant. This Promised Land is a metaphor of the New Covenant. The New Covenent, which is better than the Old Covenant (Hebrews 8:6), contains a double portion. Accordingly, we have a double portion of all the blessings and anointings in the Old Testament.

Therefore, we need to connect our born-again experience to that covenant relationship so we receive everything that is His, which has now been given to us. The will of God has been read, and in the new will, He commands us to be blessed. Thus, when we refer to the prosperity of His blessings, we are talking about every area of our lives: abundance of His love, abundance of joy, abundance of His divine nature operating in our lives, abundance of power, abundance of anointing, abundance of friendship with God, and abundance of goods. God, in His goodness, lavishes His abundance on us.

*And the LORD shall make thee plenteous in goods.*
(Deuteronomy 28:11, KJV)

*The LORD shall open unto thee his good treasure.*
(Deuteronomy 28:12, KJV)

*The blessing of the LORD brings wealth.*
(Proverbs 10:22)

## We Share in His Wealth

We share in the wealth of the kingdom.

*...giving thanks to the Father, who has qualified you to share in the inheritance of the saints in the kingdom of light. For he has rescued us from the dominion of darkness and brought us into the kingdom of the Son he loves.* (Colossians 1:12-13)

God Himself qualifies us to share in the inheritance. He does this in Genesis 3 when He announces the coming Savior to Adam and Eve. He prophesies the Redeemer that will come, and throughout the Scriptures, the prophetic Word foreshadows the Lamb of God who is our substitute, taking our lack as He becomes the curse on the cross.

*Christ redeemed us from the curse of the law by becoming a curse for us, for it is written:*

*"Cursed is everyone who is hung on a tree." He redeemed us in order that the blessing given to Abraham might come to the Gentiles...* (Galatians 3:13-14)

Jesus defeated the curse of lack on the cross, and brought us into the abundant life. He qualified us to inherit the blessings of Abraham. He is the one who connects us to the will of God and says that God's will is ours.

In rescuing us from darkness, Jesus brought us into the kingdom of light. We are not to live in the darkness anymore; we are not to remain in lack. We live in a kingdom of abundance. Jesus collected all the blessings for us, and now He is giving them to us.

Jesus is the Word. It is as though He is saying, "Come on. We are in covenant agreement. Whatever is mine is flowing into you; whatever is mine becomes flesh, as I became flesh, and dwell among you." The Word is light and life. We are living in eternal life where all the knowledge that ever was, or ever will be, is present.

God sends His Word, and the Word has the Spirit of God without limit. His Word is boundless. Consequently, when we enter the kingdom of light and come into agreement with the Word, the Holy Spirit can then build that Word within us. The Spirit can reveal to us all the knowledge that ever was or ever will be. The Spirit and the Word will reveal to us the treasures that are in Christ and the mysteries of God.

His Word contains everything that we need. Yet, the cares and worries of the world consume us because we spend so little time in the Word. The devil knows what will be accomplished as we grasp the Word. He knows what happens when we surrender to the Word of God and receive it into our lives, agreeing with the Word and becoming a success.

> The devil wants to keep us in lack, caught up in worry, distracted by fear.

We will come into the genuine success of God and bring forth His express will, the power and abundance of the Almighty. Then, we will bring glory to His name.

The devil wants to keep us in lack, caught up in worry, and distracted by fear and loss. The devil would render us ineffective. If we lack love, we will enter into envy. If we lack finances, we enter into greed. If we lack health, we enter into sickness. These worries and cares come to steal the Word. The Bible says that worry and care make the Word unproductive in our lives. Worries choke out the Word and eliminate the positive. As a result, negative words come from our mouths, sowing seeds of negative thought and reaping the unfavorable harvest. Lack is a poison, a destructive force of the enemy. We have to literally hate lack.

**God Has Dreams and Visions for Us**

Opposed to the kingdom of lack, we are surrounded with abundance in the kingdom of God, the abundant source of milk and honey. When we choose to live in the kingdom of light, abundance encompasses us, touches us, and moves within our lives. We are overtaken, overwhelmed, and consumed by the blessings. This is the life that God intends for us and sees us enjoying. He does not see any less for us. God is in agreement with the written Word; it is His testament to us.

> *You crown the year with your bounty,*
> *and your carts overflow with abundance.*
> (Psalm 65:11)

> *The LORD will send a blessing on your barns and on everything you put your hand to. The LORD your God will bless you in the land he is giving you.* (Deuteronomy 28:8)

> *The LORD will open the heavens, the storehouse of his bounty, to send rain on your land in season and to bless all the work of your hands. You will lend to many nations but will borrow from none.* (Deuteronomy 28:12)

God's dream and vision for us exceeds our imagination. Stop and think about it. Imagine

lending to nations. We can perhaps imagine lending to a neighbor, but do we really believe we will
lend to nations?

According to Psalm 36:8, we feast on the abundance of God's house. Such feasting indicates that a
vast reserve exists. This verse continues with a "drink
from your river of delights." These delights indicate a
celebration. Entering into the truth of God's Word and
His abundance releases immeasurable love. Celebration, thanksgiving, gratitude, and joy explode within
us, because we have entered into God's supernatural
realm. God parties; He is celebrating. He is not sad,
and He expects us to drink of Him. We get so high on
God that we have fun serving Him.

When I first got saved, I got so high on God
that I felt I had to be scraped off the ceiling. I was so
intoxicated with God that I could not take coffee and
God at the same time. Anyone who knocked at my
door, whatever the reason, I would ask them, "Do you
know Jesus?" Sometimes they would run.

People thought I was strange, but I was just
drinking from the river of His delights. What happens
to all that celebration we have when we first get saved?
We stop drinking at the river of His delights. We quit
thinking as He thinks. We start agreeing with the enemy. We begin to believe the cares and the worries.
Then we enter back into that from which He set us
free. One day, we wake up unhappy. What changed
in us? Our agreement!

We see everything by the "eye" of faith. When we enter the Word, confess the Word, and ask the Holy Spirit to give us God's vision, thoughts, and perspective, we see with the "eye" of faith. Then, we begin to encounter everything we observe in the kingdom of God. Once we remove the sin from our eyes, the abundance comes into view. We see everything with the "eye" of faith, and we see that God has no lack.

To put it more precisely, there never has been, nor will there ever be, a lack of anything in the king- dom of God except the lack within ourselves. Any lack in the believer's life comes from inside the believer. This deficiency or need may be the result of the way the person was raised, what the parents said to the person, or generational curses. Regardless of where a person has bonded to the lack in his life, that person must get rid of that image and receive God's vision for abundant life.

Today, as I was preparing a message on the abundance, I thought about the lovely home we are in that God had previously told us to buy. We sold our home and we were in the process of looking for a new home when God led us to the house He wanted us to buy. He told us to look in the upper middle class neighborhoods for our new home. We believed God and stepped into His will for our lives, confronting the lack within us that tried to tell me we would be house-poor, lacking furniture, food, and comforts just to make the house payment. However, we said "yes" to the Word and received the beautiful home that in the natural we probably could not have afforded.

At times, I felt embarrassed and out-of-place. I felt people would recognize that I did not belong with "rich" people, but I wanted to obey God. If I wanted to please God, I had to look in the beautiful neighborhood, and I had to call my poverty mentality a sin and crucify it daily.

We found the house, and the anointing was all over us, so we bought it.

> Any lack in the believer's life comes from inside the believer.

I found out that our payments were actually lower than what we had been previously paying. The taxes were a hundred dollars less, the house payment was a hundred dollars less, and we saved an additional hundred dollars by not having a pool payment. That left us three hundred dollars more that we could use for the kingdom of God. God's abundance, therefore, is to produce more and more for us to give promotion of His kingdom worldwide. God blessed us with a gorgeous new home in a social status that was beyond what I was used to living.

My husband, Tom, was raised in poverty and it used to influence everything we did. We used to take vacations at the bargain hotel, eating at the cheapest restaurants. When God brought us out of the poverty, we started to go to the best places, the best resorts. When it was all said and done, we actually spent less money at the best places. Thinking in God's way changes our lives in awesome measures.

**Do the Word**

> *Do not merely listen to the word, and so deceive yourselves. Do what it says. Anyone who listens to the word but does not do what it says is like a man who looks at his face in a mirror and, after looking at himself, goes away and immediately forgets what he looks like. But the man who looks intently into the perfect law that gives freedom, and continues to do this, not forgetting what he has heard, but doing it—he will be blessed in what he does.* (James 1:22-25)

We cannot change ourselves, but God can change us through our coming into agreement with the Word, thinking it, and saying it. We have to make some decisions right now to leave the place we are in spiritually and go on to that which God is showing us. I ask the Holy Spirit to show me every time I have a thought of poverty or lack, so I can repent and exchange that thought for God's thoughts. If we are ever going to come into the abundant life that Jesus has given us, it is absolutely essential that we:

- Think It          (Matthew 12:34)
- See It            (2 Corinthians 4:18)
- Speak It          (Romans 4:17)
- Write It          (Habbakkuk 2:2)
- Do It             (James 2:26)

Years ago, we learned that God is our source; the church is not our source. There was a time when we did not own a car. When we lived in Wisconsin, Tom had to walk in 20 below zero weather to the grocery store to bring home food for our two babies. At that time, he was a principal of a Christian school with an income near $7,000 a year.

So, we began to say "yes" to the Word of the Lord. We could not look at the circumstance of not having a car. Instead, we looked at what God said, and in the morning we would pray for God to lead us daily with benefits. We prayed that we would lack nothing of value and for no good thing to be withheld from us. We prayed for wealth and riches in our home. I quoted the Word and did my little charismatic dance around the kitchen at the beginning of the day. If Tom would say we were short in our finances, we would get a prosperity tape and play it to hear the Scriptures.

One time, when we were five hundred dollars short on our bills, Tom and I went for a walk and prayed in the spirit quoting the prosperity scriptures out loud. We told no one, for as we were speaking, the peace of God consumed us and we were overtaken by joy. The following Sunday, someone came up to Tom and said, "The Lord said to give you this envelope." That particular envelope contained five hundred dollars. Tom cried with tears of joy and rejoiced all the way home, reliving the greatness of God. What would have happened if we had agreed with our circumstance of depression, worry and fear?

We do not look at what we see; instead, we look at what we do not see. What we see is temporary; what we do not see is eternal. Every Scripture has God's vision behind it; God is a visionary. We should have His movie in mind whenever we sit down with the Word. We can let Him put the video on the screen, and we can enter in and live with Him. He prepares a table for us in the presence of our enemies. From which table do you eat? The table of blessings or the table of enemies?

We quote the Word aloud because God calls those things that are not as though they were. We write it down to remind us that it is done. Writing keeps us focused on what we should think, rather than what we do think. We do the Word because faith without works is dead. If God says to get a gorgeous new home in a rich neighborhood, you just do it.

**Learn to Receive**

There are literally thousands upon thousands of honest, good, and hard-working Christians who labor diligently and do everything right, but never come into the abundant life. They work from early morning to late at night, laboring and laboring without coming out of lack, because they do not know how to receive from God. The seed cannot produce if it is not received into the heart.

As we were coming out of poverty and over the last seventeen years, I compiled a book of Scriptures that I confess aloud. I ask the Holy Spirit to give me Scriptures to receive relating to my needs. I then say the Scriptures, think them, and see myself living in those Scriptures. Once I see it, it is planted in my heart, and

> We do not look at what we see; instead we look at what we do not see.

I then know that I have come into covenant with the Word of God and have truly received it. Next, I say it, call it forth, and write it down. Finally, the Holy Spirit shows me what to do, if I need to do something.

Many times people do not know how to receive from God. When our son, Scot, was sixteen, he spent time looking for a job, but he could not get one. So we sat down and prayed.

We told him, "Scot, receive your job."

"Well, how do I receive the job?" he asked.

"Just ask the Holy Spirit now," we said. The Lord told us to tell him to see the word "job" and to see God giving it to him.

Scot did just that; he saw the word "job" handed to him, and in doing so, he received it in his heart.

He saw himself working. We wrote it down, and the next day when I came home, I asked Scot if he got his job.

"Oh, yeah, I got my job," he said.

"Well, where are you working?" I asked.

"I've got my job in here," he gestured toward his chest. "It's done. I got my job."

It seemed as though he was telling me not to tempt him to say anything contrary to what he received in his heart.

The next day, he got a job that he kept all the way through high school, and it was a total blessing to him.

The devil wants to keep us from receiving. He wants us to stop short and not learn to develop receiving in the kingdom of God. If you have never spent time receiving and seeing it done, then it is hard to break that barrier.

People do not know how to receive from God (Mark 11:24). Their belief system is in lack (James 1:22-23), and they do not know how to die daily to that lack within them (Colossians 3:1-3). They do not know how to lose their life to find it (Matthew 16:24-25).

People who do not receive believe in lack. They think lack, they meditate on lack, they see lack and they behave in lack. Their belief system is in lack. We see this with Peter, who fishes all night believing in lack. Then, Jesus comes to his boat and tells him to let down his net on the other side in the daytime. Peter knows that catching fish in the daytime is an impossibility, because the waters are so clear that the fish see the net. Yet, Peter chooses to do the Word. He lets down his net and God fills it to an overabundance. Peter's boat nearly sinks from the weight of the fish.

A human body is comprised of millions upon millions of cells, and each of them is influenced in its movement by thought, vision, and speaking. The body responds to whatever we think, see, or say. If we think peaceful thoughts, we might relax. If we entertain worrisome, fearful thoughts, we might become physically tense. When we begin to hold thoughts of blessing, success, and increase, we will respond physically and mentally to these thoughts.

Consequently, we develop an understanding of the ways in which we have been conditioned, of why we are getting the results we get, and of how we can change our beliefs or conditioning. The probable reason so few people ever actually succeed is that they do not commit to change. Nonetheless, change occurs with discipline and repentance; thus, diligent effort and knowledge of God's ways produce a reversal of misfortunes in our lives.

## 4
### No Lack in God's Kingdom

The power to do the impossible lives within us. The Bible says that the same spirit that raised Christ from the dead dwells within us (Romans 8:11). God has not withheld His power; He has lavished His power upon us. We are to come into agreement with that power, for it is the key to resolving the lack in our lives. It brings us into the truth of God's Word. Whether we feel like it or not, our destiny is not our feelings, but rather what the Word of God says it is.

God does not lack. "Lack" is not even in His vocabulary. God knows only abundance.

*In the last days, God says,*
*I will pour out my Spirit on all people.*
*Your sons and daughters will prophesy,*
*your young men will see visions,*
*your old men will dream dreams.*
(Acts 2:17)

Old men will dream dreams, and there will be prophecies between the sons and the daughters and the Spirit of the Lord. They will have vision. We realize God has poured out His Spirit abundantly in each of

us, and then we understand that the breath of God, his
Spirit, is there to lead us into all victory and power. We
"overflow with abundance" (Psalm 65:11). We have
more power than we need.

The kingdom of God is within us. As Jesus said,
"nor will people say, 'Here it is,' or 'There it is,' because
the kingdom of God is within you" (Luke 17:21). We
are citizens of heaven, members of the household of
God, subjects in His kingdom. The fullness of God
lives within us.

> *Do you not know that your body is a temple
> of the Holy Spirit, who is in you, whom you
> have received from God? You are not your
> own.* (1 Corinthians 6:19)

You are the house of God. Your body is that which
houses the Spirit of the Living God and your spirit. The
power to do the impossible resides within you.

The soul of a person comprises the mind,
the will, the emotions, and the subconscious. The
"spirit-man" lives in the subconscious. This is the
heart of a person's being—the subconscious and the
"spirit-man." Because God made us this way, the
Bible says:

> *For the word of God is living and active. Sharp-
> er than any double-edged sword, it penetrates
> even to dividing soul and spirit, joints and mar-*

*row; it judges the thoughts and attitudes of the heart."* (Hebrews 4:12)

The Word of God reveals the thoughts and intents of our hearts. Excavated and exposed by the Word, the hidden images, attitudes, and beliefs of the heart are juxtaposed to God's thoughts. Those beliefs and attitudes which are in conflict with the Holy Spirit are to be removed by the believer and supplanted with right thoughts, coming into agreement with the "spirit-man" and with the Spirit of Almighty God.

We have a physical body in which the "spirit-man" and the Holy Spirit dwell. We also have a soul which has collected significant quantities of junk over the years, along with inheriting the sinful tendencies of our forefathers. This trash, which is contrary to the Word of God, stays in us and fights against God's plans for our lives. It keeps us in poverty in every area of our lives: marriage, finances, emotions, physical health, or whatever can be named.

When I talk about the prosperity of the Lord, I am not talking about greed.

*For the sake of the house of the LORD our God,*
*I will seek your prosperity.*
(Psalm 122:9)

God has a prosperity that is holy and righteous, and it is His nature to give to us what He has.

The prosperity increases as God gives. Moreover, we have no end of increase as we give.

*The lions may grow weak and hungry,*
*but those who seek the LORD lack no good*
*thing.*

(Psalm 34:10)

On the other hand, greed says to hold onto what we have, to horde our goods. A wealthy person in greed might live as though poor by not enjoying their affluence. Greedy persons do not own wealth, but rather their riches possess them. The Bible says the spirit of greed is idolatry, a love of self.

As we step into prosperity, the Holy Spirit may reveal some buds of greed or sources of generational inheritance of greed for us to remove. When such sins are revealed by God, we just get rid of the sin and do not allow it to control us anymore.

The subconscious mind is like a computer. It stores every belief we have ever had. All things considered, it is amazing that at the mere touch of a button, this entire book can be read on a computer screen, page after page. Years from now, the computer can still not only remember the book as it was loaded into the computer, but it will also be ready at any moment to edit or change the book. Even more fascinating to me, are the programs preset into the hard drive on my computer. In addition to reading the book, the computer remembers the patterns by which it retrieves information, calculates numbers, and regulates an internal clock on a daily basis.

In a similar manner, we have preset patterns in our subconscious—patterns of lack, self-destructive behaviors, and self-centeredness. These beliefs can be idols that rise up and automatically run our lives for us. To break these patterns, we want to change the belief system within us that is less than God wants it to be.

> The spirit of greed is idolatry, a love of self.

### How to Change Our Hard Drives

How do we change our "hard drives?" First, we repent. As Paul says, we must die daily (1 Corinthians 15:31). Paul dealt with sin in his life daily by seeing the sin crucified with Christ. He saw it dead and buried, and he received resurrection life in himself to renew righteousness in place of sin. This application of the whole Gospel to the believer's life is the act of repentance.

A dead person cannot sin, so a believer must die to sin. Paul died to anything in himself that was contrary to the Word of God. We must also, according to the Bible, develop the habit of putting the misdeeds or sinful patterns of the flesh to death by the power of the Spirit of God. Paul saw that his old man of flesh was crucified in Christ and powerless to control him, because he visualized it nailed to the cross with its passions and desires. Such repentance will break the power of lack.

This repentance actually keeps us from focusing on sin or becoming "sin-conscious." In the Old Testament, God tells His people to break down idols and destroy them. When we repent at the cross, we destroy the idols or patterns of sin hidden in the subconscious.

The second action we take in ridding ourselves of a belief system that is less than what God provides for us is to form new thoughts. We must, as Paul did, go on to the resurrection experience. Once sin (the old pattern of thinking) is removed, it must be replaced with a new image, a new word, or a new thought inside of us. We receive what God says, come into agreement with the resurrection, and form new thoughts.

Next, we form a new vision, after the old one was destroyed with the power of the Holy Spirit. Now we receive the image of what the Word of God says about us. The Bible says that Jesus is the image of the invisible God (Hebrews 1:3). He is the Word of God, and all the promises of God are settled forever in Christ. God knows that we live with the condemnation that comes from the enemy that persecutes our souls. The enemy tries in every way to get us to believe that we are less than what God says. But God says His promises are established. God no longer cares what we have done in the past, because He has forgiven us and put away the memory of it. We must receive His Word as the vision of God for us.

Think of areas where you have lack: finances, health, job, marriage, energy, children. Lack can be in any area that you are not living in the fullness of the abundance of God and what God, according to His Word, has ordained for your life. What image do you have inside of you? Do you have the image of what God says? Are you finding the Scriptures that say His abundance in those areas?

> The enemy tries in every way to get us to believe that we are less than what God says.

Are you beginning to take on that thought as the truth? Are you beginning to put the new picture inside you?

We have the resurrection power of God within us. We cannot stand before God and say, "The family I was born in kept me in lack," or "It was the way I was raised." With the same Spirit that raised Christ from the dead living within us, we cannot excuse ourselves from making the effort to receive God's image for us. In addition, new speech patterns must occur to change a destructive belief system. We make a decision to speak new thoughts and to call forth God's vision.

### For the Love of Christ

The love of Christ that is within us must be the motive for abundance and a new way of speaking in every aspect of our lives. That love needs to go out for

His people. In every situation, it should be the love of Christ that is compelling us, holding us together, and keeping us going.

I know that when the enemy hit me with incurable rheumatoid arthritis several years ago, it was the love of Christ that compelled me to grasp all of God's healing. That is what sustained me as I pressed on into complete healing. If I had not received the miracle of divine health I had been preaching about, it could have affected the destiny of many. My choosing to go about in a wheel chair—through love of self more than the love of Christ—could have affected you and your children and grandchildren.

The love of Christ is what healed me. Our motive for God's abundance lies not in greed, but in wanting to see others receive His abundance. We want to be a testimony to our neighbors that God is good all the time. What neighbor of yours will want Jesus if all kinds of atrocities are happening to you? They might say to you, "I don't want to get involved with your God. I've got enough problems in my life!"

> *For Christ's love compels us, because we are convinced that one died for all, and therefore all died. And he died for all, that those who live should no longer live for themselves but for him who died for them and was raised again. (2 Corinthians 5:14-15)*

In an abundant life, we do not live for ourselves any more. Our lives are hidden in God. Being bought with the precious blood of Jesus, we are not our own. We must face the fact that in order to come into abundance, we must lose our lives that we might gain them. As long as a person tries to hold onto his life, he will lose all that he has.

### Repetition Will Produce

Any good or bad idea, plan, or purpose may be planted in the subconscious mind by repetition of thought, vision, or speech, and it will be empowered by faith and expectancy. Suppose a person hears a negative report from a doctor, or that his children have not arrived home yet from a long trip. The person who hears such a report will usually envision the worst scenario and begin to expend effort on resolving the worst thing that could happen. If we allow ourselves to similarly dwell on the worst outcomes, we are planting ideas and purposes in our subconscious that produce a negative image. Let's call that negative image an idol, because it occupies our focus and stands against the Word of God. The Bible says that care and worry choke out the Word of God; problem-solving can be very non-productive in our lives.

> *When tempted, no one should say, "God is tempting me." For God cannot be tempted by evil, nor does he tempt anyone; but each one is tempted*

*when, by his own evil desire, he is dragged away and enticed. Then, after desire has conceived, it gives birth to sin; and sin, when it is full-grown, gives birth to death.* (James 1:13-15)

God wants us to see that when a bad idea is planted in our subconscious, it can give birth inside us. Then, that idea grows, becomes sin, and brings death. Therefore, we must make a decision to master any area we are battling that is contrary to the Word of God.

*If you do what is right, will you not be accepted? But if you do not do what is right, sin is crouching at your door; it desires to have you, but you must master it.* (Genesis 4:7)

Sometimes people deal with divorce. They have problems in their marriage, and they have a small quarrel. All of a sudden, one or both start imagining how wonderful it would be to live on their own. They get a divorce, thinking life would be better without that person (the habit of imagining the worst could even be a generational sin—something that their parents and ancestors continually practiced). Then, one day, the imagined scenario is conceived in the heart. From there, the smallest incident will trigger it into action; without taking any thought, that person may jump into divorce.

Instead of recreating the worst scenario, we must make a decision to repent of the image of that scene, and develop the habit of thinking what God thinks, saying what God says, and seeing what God sees.

A person's life history can only change when he discovers this to be true and makes a conscious decision to come into agreement with God's Word. With a conscious choice, we can connect to the power that Jesus has already provided to destroy the works of the enemy, to demolish images and idols, and to connect to the Word of God.

### Covenant Agreement

I call this conscious decision "coming into covenant agreement." I say, "God, I come into covenant with your Word. We have covenant. I see the blood of Jesus on that Scripture and on me, and we are one, and I receive that as one."

Moses sprinkled the blood of a lamb (symbolic of the blood of Jesus) on the people and on the Word of God. This picture of covenant agreement in the Old Testament foreshadows our covenant of grace through Christ when we come into agreement with the Word of God. Let God be true in His Word, and let every man, or human flesh, be a liar. No matter what the circumstances are, my testimony will be the Word of God.

God says we will lend money to nations; that is His standard for us. Yet, we allow ourselves to focus on just paying the bills. Our standard for ourselves lies so far beneath His that we often fail to grasp the reality of His purpose for us.

Instead of saying, "God, please just help me pay my bills on time," we should be saying, "God, You have the power to do anything, and I agree with You that my bills are paid and I give glory to You, Almighty God. Praise You God. Thank You, God, I am in agreement with You and I know You have already performed it."

Getting involved with a new thought, vision, and speech system, along with dying daily, will lead you to discover what lies within you. You will discover the picture of what God has within you! The Word will divide soul and spirit, joints and marrow, and will reveal the thoughts and intents of your subconscious, it will also reveal the idols in your heart. Paul says:

> *So I find this law at work: When I want to do good, evil is right there with me. For in my inner being I delight in God's law; but I see another law at work in the members of my body, waging war against the law of my mind and making me a prisoner of the law of sin at work within my members...who will rescue me?... Jesus Christ our Lord!* (Romans 7:21-25)

Paul says that Jesus helped him overcome the flesh. Jesus is the Word. If God reveals His Word to us, it exposes anything in our subconscious that is not in agreement with His Word. Wrong motives and attitudes will be brought to the surface so we can get rid of those aspects of our character.

We are surrounded with the Word of God, which in turn, surrounds us with great men and women of faith and power who move in the miraculous.

*Therefore, since we are surrounded by such a great cloud of witnesses, let us throw off everything that hinders and the sin that so easily entangles, and let us run with perseverance the race marked out for us. Let us fix our eyes on Jesus, the author and perfecter of our faith, who for the joy set before him endured the cross, scorning its shame, and sat down at the right hand of the throne of God.* (Hebrews 12:1-2)

Moses parted the Red Sea, Daniel overcame the den of the lions, and Joseph saved a nation. David killed a lion, a bear, and a giant. God says we have a double portion of the same anointing of these "witnesses" through the New Covenant. We are already in the New Covenant and have therefore received a double portion of the inheritance of the anointing of the Spirit of God.

When Elijah knew it was time for him to go to meet the Lord, Elisha followed him for three days and refused to leave. Finally, Elijah asked Elisha what he wanted. Elisha asked for a double portion of the great prophet's anointing. Elijah is a picture of the Old Covenant giving way to the New Covenant. Through this picture, we see the double portion of the New Covenant we have in Christ.

*Instead of their shame*
    *my people will receive a double portion,*
*and instead of disgrace*
    *they will rejoice in their inheritance;*
*and so they will inherit a double portion in their*
        *land,*
    *and everlasting joy will be theirs.*
                        (Isaiah 61:7)

As the twelve spies sent by Joshua returned, ten had a bad report, because generation after generation had been slaves, and the images remained in their minds as descendants of downtrodden Hebrews from Egypt. The spies complained:

*"But the people who live there are powerful, and the cities are fortified and very large... We can't attack those people; they are stronger than we are... The land we explored devours those living in it. All the people we saw there are of*

*great size... We seemed like grasshoppers in
our own eyes, and we looked the same to them.*
(Numbers 13:28, 31-33)

Because of being ruled by masters who beat
them and murdered their children, the spies saw themselves as grasshoppers compared to their enemies.
They pictured themselves as slaves.

God told them to meditate daily on the signs and
wonders and on His Word. He admonished them to
see His principles and to focus on who He is. Unfortunately, the Israelites did not get around to obeying
God. Although they had physically come into the
land of abundance, their hearts and minds remained
full of the images of Egypt, and they had faith only for
living in Egypt. We, too, must deal with the images
implanted by the world, by dysfunctional families or
by tradition.

**Seek First The Kingdom of God**

We must visualize the inheritance we have
received in Jesus as being used for God's kingdom.
We receive the abundance of the inheritance, not for
personal gain, but for the kingdom of God.

*For the sake of the house of the LORD our God,
I will seek your prosperity.*
(Psalm 122:9)

*But seek first his kingdom and his righteousness,*
*and all these things will be given to you as well.*
(Matthew 6:33)

These Scriptures mean we should seek first the expansion of God's kingdom worldwide and want the kingdom to advance to all nations. The inheritance provides power far beyond the service that we are doing now in the kingdom of God. When we come into his abundance, we will also have ample energy, bountiful strength, and copious wisdom to do greater and better than we otherwise could have in the natural. Because God is able to pour his grace unto us, we will abound in every good work. In this way, we receive the abundance of the mind of Christ so we can accomplish everything more efficiently than ever before.

Receiving from Jesus should be a comfortable experience for us. We have all the tools necessary to build God's kingdom. Our surroundings are to be in agreement with God's Word. We are to create an inheritance awareness within ourselves.

Before I began to believe for the "milk and honey" existence, I had been believing for poverty, and I had quite a lot of success in receiving poverty. I was surrounded with it as an atmosphere; it was my system of belief. I spent my first years of Christian growth in tradition, surrounded by well-meaning Christians who spoke of "poverty" and "poor" and that having nothing was God's character. So, I believed for it. I was taught that God made people sick and beat them up just to make them better people.

I think the devil might have said, "Boy, there's an open door at her house. I can have a field day with this. We can go in there any time with oppression, sickness, depression, or poverty."

But the Holy Spirit says, "There's a better way."

In order to walk in the abundant life that Jesus

> I had been believing for poverty, and I had quite a lot of success in receiving poverty.

talks about and has provided, we need to create an awareness of our inheritance. Without faith, we cannot please God, so it is necessary for us to be aware of what we believe. Such faith is the act of believing not only that He exists, but also that He rewards. Once we become aware, we begin to see abundance everywhere.

> *And without faith it is impossible to please God, because anyone who comes to him must believe that he exists and that he rewards those who earnestly seek him.* (Hebrews 11:6)

### Commitment Time

Now is the time to make a commitment, because once we decide to change, God will change us and make His abundance a reality in our lives. Lack and limitations can only exist when we make room for them in our minds and in our speech. If we choose the luxury of relaxing our faith and allowing our thoughts to be occupied with lack, then we reap that impoverishment in our lives. The flesh loves to be in charge of us in this way; the flesh chooses laziness over the effort of focusing our faith in His abundance.

Resolve now to completely remove the image of lack and of limitation of abilities from your mind and understand the inheritance God has given to you. Abundant life has already been given you; you must possess it.

*I can do everything through him who gives me strength.* (Philippians 4:13)

Now, believe to receive it. Begin immediately to exercise faith in God's Word. Get into the habit of visualizing yourself in possession of abundant life.

Let the Holy Spirit show you some of the improvements and increases you would have with the inheritance you have received, and then start confessing aloud that you already have these increased aspects.

*Since we live by the Spirit, let us keep in step with the Spirit.* (Galatians 5:25)

Because the subconscious mind cannot tell the difference between actually doing something and merely visualizing an act, repeating aloud the Scripture's promises of abundance creates an awareness for increase.

> *Now faith is being sure of what we hope for and certain of what we do not see.* (Hebrews 11:1)

Let God develop within you a receiving heart of faith.

# 5
## Meditation on God's Word: The Key to Success

In our early years of Christianity, my husband Tom and I were in the Bahamas listening to a world-famous evangelist preach, and I became increasingly more angry with what I heard at each meeting. The message hit every ounce of religiosity and traditionalism within me. The preacher said such a terrible thing. He said God is materialistic. Can you believe it?

Then, the preacher went on to explain that God has streets of gold. Our most precious metal here on earth is mere pavement to God. What a week for me! God used this precious servant of His to break the deadly traditions that were rooted deeply in me. It was a very hard week on my flesh, but the Word of God set me free.

We tend to get angry when the traditional religiosity within us is confronted by someone God is sending (someone to break down the comfort zone of our preset boundaries). It is as though God tells us, "In faith there are no limits." Note the following Scriptures:

*In your good pleasure make Zion prosper;*
*build up the walls of Jerusalem.*
(Psalm 51:18)

*The LORD will grant you abundant prosperity.*
(Deuteronomy 28:11)

*That I may cause those that love me to inherit substance; and I will fill their treasures.* (Proverbs 8:21, KJV)

*The blessing of the LORD brings wealth.* (Proverbs 10:22)

*...the LORD your God will bless you in all your work and in everything you put your hand to.* (Deuteronomy 15:10)

*Moreover, when God gives any man wealth and possessions, and enables him to enjoy them, to accept his lot and be happy in his work—this is a gift of God.* (Ecclesiates 5:19)

*...you will be prosperous and successful.* (Joshua 1:8b)

*Blessed is the man who fears the LORD,*
*who finds great delight in his commands...*
*Wealth and riches are in his house,*
*and his righteousness endures forever.*
(Psalm 112:1, 3)

*But remember the LORD your God, for it is he who gives you the ability to produce wealth.* (Deuteronomy 8:18)

*A faithful man will be richly blessed,*
  *but one eager to get rich will not go unpunished.*
(Proverbs 28:20)

Now, read aloud these same scriptures, reworded here as personal promises:

*For the Lord has pleasure in my prosperity. The Lord will make me plenteous in goods. The blessing of the Lord brings wealth. The Lord will command his blessings upon me and all that I set my hands to. Riches and wealth are a gift of God. The Lord shall make my way prosperous and I will have good success. Blessed is everyone who fears the Lord and delights greatly in his commandments. Wealth and riches shall be in my house. I will remember the Lord my God for it is He who gives me the power to get wealth. The blessings of the Lord bring wealth. I am a faithful person and I shall abound with the blessings of God.*

If you read those aloud and believed what you were reading, then you have, in a manner, done what I call "meditating on the scriptures." Did you let the

Word get into you?  Did you let that speak to your heart?  God wants you to come into the truth of His Word.

I want to show you that the Bible conveys the importance of meditation throughout its pages.  The meaning of the word meditation in the current vernacular would be "self-talk," which means to speak either aloud or under one's breath.  At any rate, a person would definitely hear what is spoken within himself.  This conversation may take place with words, pictures, or thoughts, but it usually occurs constantly within a person.  Furthermore, it creates an image within us that our subconscious agrees with or our heart adheres to.

**Meditation; a Life Changer**

True meditation is a life changer; it can change the past, the present, and the future.  Images within someone that are contrary to the Word of God are permanently replaced with new images from the Bible.  Through meditation, we can break preset boundaries and establish God's limitlessness.  Meditation is vital for every Christian.

God commands us to meditate.  I compare meditation to having a meal.  Nutritionists say that a meal of chicken, carrots, and beans would be loaded with vitamins and proteins that are essential to good physical health, but we cannot see those nutrients.  Nonetheless, we choose to eat the food.

What we eat, we become; if we eat a diet of sponge cake, we will look like sponges. To avoid this, we decide to put good food in our mouths, chew it, and swallow it. If we spit food out after chewing it, we will not benefit from it, no matter how good it is. However, once we swallow the food, we are no longer in charge of it; the body automatically takes over and digests the food.

In the same way, we decide what to think, what visions to have, and whether to agree with the Word of God or with circumstances. We decide what kind of "self-talk" we will have. When we are meditating on God's Word, it is similar to digesting. Just as body fluids mix with food to extract nutrients, so also does the Holy Spirit mix with the Word of God, extracting the life of it. All of a sudden, the subconscious grabs the Word of God and changes images planted within us. This then brings us into agreement with God's Word and releases faith so that the Word can become flesh and eternally dwell within.

Meditation can change the history of your life. God says He promises prosperity and success if we meditate on His Word.

> *Do not let this Book of the Law depart from your mouth; meditate on it day and night, so that you may be careful to do everything written in it. Then you will be prosperous and successful.* (Joshua 1:8)

Do not let the words of God vanish from your mouth. Once the Word gets inside you, it has the power to bring your subconscious into agreement with God's plan, will, and purpose for your life. Prosperity and success will dominate your life.

## Make Tapes

One time, years ago, when I was at a convention, I found myself flooded with negative thoughts. I feared that I would come to the church we were pastoring and find that it was empty. I was overwhelmed with these thoughts in the night. It seems ironic that it could happen in such a setting. The enemy likes to attack in the night when we are asleep or when we have let down our defenses. Because the confession of God's Word is so powerful, it is important to make tapes of our own voices speaking scriptures of blessings, prosperity and abundance in every area so that we will immerse ourselves in His standard for our lives.

Now, as I wake in the night, I hear myself on tape speaking God's Word. I immediately experience myself stepping into His promises of abundance and blessing, and I let the Word planted in me rise up and conquer the strongholds with which the enemy wanted me to agree. Though I had momentarily experienced the oppression of the enemy, by morning I was in the victory of abundance and success in all of God's goodness according to His Word.

*My eyes stay open through the watches of the*
*    night,*
*    that I may meditate on your promises.*
(Psalm 119:148)

The enemy attempts to drown us in all sorts of negative thoughts such as divorce, failure, or loss of income. Though the adversary attacks us with pictures of defeat, poverty, lack, and destruction, we can draw from our agreement with the Word, from the Holy Spirit, and from the images we have built in our hearts. In this way, the power of the enemy is broken.

> I let the Word planted in me rise up and conquer the strongholds that the enemy wanted me to agree with.

But, if we meditate on the thoughts of the enemy, and if we keep the negative images in our mouths, then those destructive fears will become a reality. What we meditate, we get.

*Blessed is the man…*
*[whose] delight is in the law of the LORD,*
*    and on his law he meditates day and night.*
*He is like a tree planted by streams of water,*
*    which yields fruit in season*
*and whose leaf does not wither.*
*    Whatever he does prospers.*
(Psalm 1:1-3)

God does not lie. If we wake up quoting His Word, we will prosper in all that we do, including breaking repeating incidents (cycles) of abuse, illness, addiction, or divorce. Writing out the promises of God for your situation will help you in saying or meditating the covenant guarantees of God's Word aloud.

I have written a book, Confessing God's Word, in which the scriptures are specially written for meditation and are listed in categories, such as "Marriage," "Peace," "Healing" and "Prosperity." We turn to the pages that address our particular need or "lack" and use those pages for daily meditation. Suppose a person grabs the book and uses it to begin each day in covenant agreement with God's Word. The seed of God, which is planted and nurtured by meditation, will produce after its own kind in that person.

At about 3:00 A.M. the other night, I woke up and lay awake a long time seeing piles of wealth and riches in my house. What a contrast to that other experience years ago at the same time of night when I had imagined an empty church building! As I saw the wealth and riches, I began to think of ways to give it away. I realized that I needed more money coming in because I wanted to give so much more away.

Remember the preacher I was listening to in the Bahamas? He was speaking of this kind of generosity when he said, "Today, because I've stepped into the promises of God, I now give $80,000 a year away into the kingdom."

Obviously, this man blesses and expands the kingdom of God. Think about who is to do the giving. Do you think members of organized crime will support the kingdom of God financially? God intends for His children to give into the kingdom for the sake of the house of the Lord.

**Steps to Take**

This generosity is not only for financial support, but also for any area of life in which we lack something. There are steps that we take to apply this truth.

First, a person needs to understand that every human talks to himself. Each of us speaks within his or her mind or heart. Some people, like my mother, do it aloud. I often think aloud, too, in order to sort things out. If you are one who thinks at all, you also need to be thinking the Word of God and speaking of blessings rather than verbally rehearsing and reliving some bad situation that has already happened or that you fear may happen.

Isaac meditated in a field (Genesis 24:63). Involved in a private conversation with himself, he looked up and saw Rebekah for the first time. He immediately married her, thus, illustrating that people can bring themselves into the plan of God through meditating on the scriptures. Isaac knew that his father, Abraham, had sent a servant to get him a wife. I am sure that Isaac was meditating in agreement with the Word of God and believing God for the very best that He had for him.

God calls us to be actively involved in His plans for our lives. We are to always speak what the Bible says about God, about ourselves and others, and about life. Contrast the following thoughts from Psalms with some of the statements that have rolled off your tongue.

*Within your temple, O God,*
    *we meditate on your unfailing love.*
            **(Psalm 48:9)**

*I will meditate on all your works*
    *and consider all your mighty deeds.*
            **(Psalm 77:12)**

In a vision, I saw a human tongue stuck to the cross. By this vision, I understood that leaving our tongues at the cross, mortifying the deeds of the flesh, is the only way to dominate our speech. The Book of James says that the tongue can destroy like a wild fire and that the tongue cannot be tamed, meaning through human effort. Human flesh cannot restrain its evil. But, if you will see your tongue stuck on the cross where the curse was, then the cross will contain the tongue. The Bible says we're to have a tight rein on our tongues. A person that doesn't is of little worth. When we believe that we have crucified the tongue with the flesh, there is a tight control on the tongue, and we purify its use through meditation on the Word. This cleanses and frees the tongue to serve only God.

In contrast, the devil works on human conversation, because his only power is granted through the negatives we speak.

*The tongue has the power of life and death,*
*and those who love it will eat its fruit.*
(Proverbs 18:21)

If we are connected to the love of the negative, we will eat the fruit of our speech—death. As the Scripture says, "we meditate on your unfailing love" (Psalm 48:9). We are told to spend time talking aloud to ourselves about the immeasurable, unfailing love of God for us in the death, burial, and resurrection of Christ. After all, there is no greater love than that of a man laying down his life for another (John 15:13). So, we meditate on the works of Christ and on His becoming

> We meditate on visualizing ourselves walking the same path and living the same lifestyle as Christ lived.

sin for us that we can now be the righteousness of God (2 Corinthians 5:21). We meditate on Christ's defeat of the designs of the adversary. We meditate on Christ taking on all the curses of the law and sin so that we can be free to receive the blessings of God.

We emerge from the kingdom of darkness into the kingdom of life and abundance. We meditate on visualizing ourselves walking the same path and living the same lifestyle as Christ lived. We do this by meditating on His love, on how much He cares for us, and by seeing that God received us by faith into the family of God.

We meditate or speak aloud positive confessions of our health and our prosperity. He sent His Word to heal us. He became poor that we might become rich.

> *Wealth and riches are in his house,*
>     *and his righteousness endures forever.*
>                 (Psalm 112:3)

In His wealth and in His riches life becomes pure and holy. Talk of how good God is and thank Him for who He is. When you declare that God "is good; and his love endures forever" (Psalm 118:1), and when your subconscious is in accord with your words, you will begin to see truth and life the way God sees reality, and His presence and glory will fill your body which is the temple of the soul and spirit.

### The Greatest Joy is in Experiencing God

The greatest joy is in experiencing God. When we sense doubt and unbelief, that is the time to meditate on the promises of God.

> *They will speak of the glorious splendor of your*
>     *majesty,*

*and I will meditate on your wonderful
works.*
(Psalm 145:5)

David, the great worshiper and psalmist, meditates on the wonders of God in the book of Psalms. Imagine David out on a hillside watching the sheep at night and enjoying the stars.

*They will tell of the power of your awesome
works,
and I will proclaim your great deeds.*
(Psalm 145:6)

As he admires the stars above, the "awesome works," what he proclaims speaking aloud are the great deeds of God. Who hears David speak aloud? David. Whose destiny is conformed to the will of God? David's. David, a truly ordinary human, knew to "meditate the wonders of God," because he recognized the power of the spoken Word of God—power over his own mind, will, emotions and subconscious.

David meditates on the promises and glorifies the Lord in all He has done, and one day, David becomes King of Israel. Let's see what God had to say about David shortly before David was anointed king by Samuel.

*...the* Lord *has sought out a man after his own heart and appointed him leader of his people...*
(1 Samuel 13:14)

How did David develop a heart that God says is like His own?  He develops this kind of heart by meditating on the thoughts, intents, and purposes of God as found in His Word.

In meditating, we call those things that are not as though they were (Romans 4:17). If we were ill, we would not deny the illness, but instead we would call forth health.  If our marriages were troubled, we would meditate, speak, and proclaim that our spouses are a blessing (Proverbs 18:22), are filled with godly wisdom (Proverbs 31:26 Amp), and love as Christ loves the church (Ephesians 5: 2 5).  If our finances are destroyed, we proclaim our wealth and abundance in Him.

We speak of God's goals for our families, ourselves, and the church as we meditate aloud.  In the New Covenant, we have a double portion of God's abundance.  We must agree with His covenant.  No matter what happens, continually say, "God has called us into a supernatural abundance."

*Till I come, give attendance to reading, to exhortation, to doctrine. Neglect not the gift that is in thee, which was given thee by prophecy, with the laying on of the hands of the presbytery.*

*Meditate upon these things; give thyself wholly
to them; that thy profiting may appear to all.*
(1 Timothy 4:13-15, KJV)

God wants us to meditate on those things that were deposited within us as we became Christians (those gifts planted through prophetic anointing, through the elders laying hands on us, or through the Holy Spirit). We are to give ourselves diligently to these things and meditate on the Word of God relating to these gifts.

Making a commitment right now to meditate on the Word of God is the wisest thing we can do.

*May my meditation be pleasing to him,
    as I rejoice in the LORD.*
                (Psalm 104:34)

*May the words of my mouth and the meditation
    of my heart
    be pleasing in your sight,
    O LORD, my Rock and my Redeemer.*
                (Psalm 19:14)

Such meditation is pleasing to God. It highlights and develops God's potential for us. Meditation on the Word changes the course of our lives and breaks dysfunctional cycles.

*Be imitators of God, therefore, as dearly loved children and live a life of love, just as Christ loved us and gave himself up for us as a fragrant offering and sacrifice to God.* (Ephesians 5:1-2)

The wisest decision Tom and I ever made occurred about twenty years ago when we decided to agree with God's Word that we have covenant with Him. We recognized that His Word is our standard and that we would no longer live by our own testimony of experiences. We now live in the abundance of God's kingdom, but it took twenty years to get here. Now, God is calling us to step higher in His grace and lend to nations.

**Let's Change**

It takes great devotion and commitment to change the course of our history and to break a set cycle of dysfunctional behavior and unbelief. God will change whatever has been passed down from your forefathers, such as consequences of wrong decisions, and beliefs that you are less than what He says you are. Once you want to be pleasing to Him, you will want your meditation—the words of your mouth—to be in complete accord with His Word.

God is our Rock. He will protect us. He is our Redeemer. He will turn our lives into good and make us better than before.

I come from a family of wealth. My grandfather had a huge newspaper company, and my father was a multimillionaire who was raised with butlers and maids. But, my grandfather remarried and the inheritance went, not to his children, but to his third wife. My other grandfather was also a wealthy man. He was a famous interior decorator; however, his finances also went to his third wife.

Even though I love my grandfathers for who they are (rather than for their wealth), God told me to come out of the pride of life and receive my inheritance. God told me we had been living, at one time, merely to survive. He told me to get rid of the "survival mentality" and to claim back seven times over anything the devil stole or that was lost to sin (Leviticus 6:1-4; Exodus 22:3-7). God told me to reclaim it all, all the way back to Adam, lest I leave a door open through which the devil could continue to steal. We need to shut the door against the devil and declare to him he must pay back seven times.

> God told me to reclaim it all, all the way back to Adam.

God did not call us to be mere survivors, nor to be on the bottom. No, we are called to be above, not beneath. We are the head, not the tail. The devil is defeated, and God gives us more than enough to prevail. So, at the time that God told us to receive back what was stolen, we did not know we were going to have a church. We simply chose to obey God. God worked from His potential for us. We learned to "imitate God" through meditating on His Word. Thus, we created a new life for ourselves. The old life is gone, and God continually develops that potential within us.

We can create our future through what we say. For instance, last summer the Lord told me to claim Psalm 112:6-7 during a worship service.

> *Surely he will never be shaken;*
> *a righteous man will be remembered for-*
> *ever.*
> *He will have no fear of bad news;*
> *his heart is steadfast, trusting in the* LORD.
> (Psalm 112:6-7)

So I meditated on these scriptures and came into agreement with them for my family. I had my grandson, Laken, and he was a little fussy that day. Holly, his mother, suggested that it might be because he was cutting teeth. Naturally, we had to look in his mouth at his cute little teeth.

As Holly flipped Laken over so the light would enter his mouth, I saw something lodged in the upper roof of his mouth. Then, we examined his palette more closely. It appeared as though the skin had never fully grown over the bone at the roof of Laken's mouth. Pastor Tom, who happened to be at home, put his finger to the roof of Laken's mouth and said that whatever was there seemed hard, like a pumpkin seed.

Scot and Holly took Laken right to the urgent care emergency room. In all of this, we had plenty of time and opportunity to enter into fear and claim the negative. Yet, we refused to believe a bad report against Laken, whom we see as the anointed of God. No harm can come to him.

In the emergency room, several doctors, including a specialist, were called into look at what hospital staff were referring to as a "first." Apparently, Laken had put a plastic furniture tack or button in his mouth. Just think of God's timing. First of all, Laken had to flip the tack over just right to get it lodged in his mouth rather than swallowing it. Since the skin had already grown partially around it, it had to have been there for a week or longer. Then, consider that it did not fall into his throat while he was sleeping or playing. If it had been swallowed, it would most likely have choked him to death.

Can you see that God created a future for Laken by His word (Hebrews 11:3)?

Through meditation, we embark on a program of self-control (2 Corinthians 10:3-4). We discover the hidden man of our hearts, and we develop ourselves properly according to the Word of God with good spiritual growth.

*Therefore, rid yourselves of all malice and all deceit, hypocrisy, envy, and slander of every kind.* (1 Peter 2:1)

We no longer think as we used to think. We make decisions to have a tight rein on our tongues and a guard on our thoughts.

Meditation makes a person aware that he is comprised of three parts. There is a spirit, a soul, and a body. The Holy Spirit will show a person what is truly happening in the mind, will and emotions—the soul of man. By meditating, we allow ourselves to be controlled by what the Bible says.

> *Therefore I do not run like a man running aimlessly; I do not fight like a man beating the air. No, I beat my body and make it my slave so that after I have preached to others, I myself will not be disqualified for the prize.* (1 Corinthians 9:26-27)

By confessing the Scriptures aloud, we no longer run without purpose. Instead, we build the kingdom of God, and we build our bodies, which house our spirits and the Holy Spirit. We accept His vision, His pictures, and His plan. This is what we really want: to be a servant of the Most High God, to be crucified with Christ, and to lose our lives that we might gain them.

We receive divine nature from God, which has given us everything we need for life to develop self-control and make right choices.

*His divine power has given us everything we need for life and godliness through our knowledge of him who called us by his own glory and goodness. Through these he has given us his very great and precious promises, so that through them you may participate in the divine nature and escape the corruption in the world caused by evil desires.* (2 Peter 1:3-4)

Now we build a promise full of plans and ideas from the Holy Spirit.

*However, as it is written:*

*"No eye has seen,*
    *no ear has heard,*
*no mind has conceived*
        *what God has prepared for those who love*
        *him"*—

*but God has revealed it to us by his Spirit.* (1 Corinthians 2:9-10)

The Spirit of God is revealing the Word to us. He tells us what to see and what to say because we are in agreement. Ideas do not form themselves. They always enter into our minds by a process, by prayer in the Holy Spirit and by interpretation (1 Corinthians 14:14-15), by thinking and seeing the thought, by meditation, and by the Holy Spirit's desires entering the soul. This exact process makes us the creative creatures that we are designed to be. Through our creativity we are to take dominion (Genesis 1: 2 6-28).

By holding new ideas or pictures in our minds, the power of God is manifested in our lives. We are working from God's potential (Romans 8:5). The spirit is involved in conforming our thought lives to God's Word. Ideas and desires from the spirit's realm invade the soul's realm. The doing of the Word influences our physical beings.

Most people look at a result in their lives and let that result dictate their thoughts. They let life's circumstances control their thoughts and change them from the positive to the negative. For example, an empty checking account leads to thoughts of loss. Meditating on these thoughts builds the concept of poverty. The idea or picture held in a person's mind determines his or her future. We call the focus on the negative a self-destructive, self-fulfilling cycle. It is not the way God has intended for us to live. Sadly, such people do not learn to be responsible for their choices and their thought lives, and they tend to blame God for their misfortunes.

*Do not be deceived: God cannot be mocked. A man reaps what he sows. The one who sows to please his sinful nature, from that nature will reap destruction; the one who sows to please the Spirit, from the Spirit will reap eternal life. Let us not become weary in doing good, for at the proper time we will reap a harvest if we do not give up.* (Galatians 6:7-9)

# 6
## A Faith Vision

*Finally, brothers, whatever is true, whatever is noble, whatever is right, whatever is pure, whatever is lovely, whatever is admirable—if anything is excellent or praiseworthy—think about such things.* (Philippians 4:8)

Biblically, meditation is an activity. "Meditation" means to mutter or to think aloud—what I call "self-talk." Meditation includes involvement of the total person: spirit, soul, and body. God promises that when we meditate, we create His kingdom on this earth, and we will be successful and prosperous in all that He has called us to do (Joshua 1:8).

God's Word commands us to meditate—think, see, speak, and talk—on His "unfailing love" (Psalm 48:9). We are to meditate on His law (Psalm 1:2), on the Word of God, and on His promises. The Bible says that in the night hours when we wake up, we are to be meditating on His promises (Psalm 119:148). The Word tells us that we should meditate on His signs and wonders, in addition to His works, (Psalm 119:27; 143:5).

God's Word gives us the thoughts, the pictures, and the words about Him, and we should come into agreement with His Word. God commands us to meditate. Make a commitment now to develop that meditation in your life, and to consciously begin the process of developing the meditation of God.

God wants us to make new, godly pictures inside ourselves. These pictures that agree with God's Word are a "faith vision." God wants us to have eyes of faith so that we can fight faith's good fight. God wants us to enter into covenant with His Word.

God does nothing outside of His Word (2 Timothy 2:13), He binds Himself to His Word. God spoke His Word and He remains in agreement with His Word; He has done His part and now He is resting.

It is up to us to agree with Almighty God. This agreement is an important aspect of doing our part so that the Word of God can happen in our lives.

Suppose Joe Schmoe makes a joint savings account (called a covenant) with himself, his wife, and the bank. The bank will not give either one of them any money until she also signs the contract. Her signature indicates her agreement to the terms of the savings account as a covenant partner with her husband and with the bank. She is entitiled to the full amount as a co-signer. We also are co-heirs with Christ, just as the wife is to her husband. We are entitled to all that Christ has, yet, none of it comes to us until we agree with the covenant and sign on the dotted line showing our agreement.

*By faith we understand that the universe was formed at God's command, so that what is seen was not made out of what was visible.* (Hebrews 11:3)

In a state of meditation, God spoke the Word and the universe was formed. He had the picture within that was formed first in the invisible place. So it is in our lives, that as we read the Word and consciously agree with Him, we are allowing the Holy Spirit to form pictures within our hearts in agreement with God's Word. Those pictures of what is invisible will become a tangible or visible reality.

> None of it comes to us until we agree with the covenant and sign on the dotted line.

Unfortunately, most Christians live and die without ever fully understanding that God commands us to meditate. Should we disobey His command? The dunamis or miracle power of God that raised Christ from the dead and which has been given to us, creates as we speak.

*Now to him who is able to do immeasurably more than all we ask or imagine, according to his power that is at work within us...* (Ephesians 3:20)

The words "all we can ask or imagine" relate to our meditating, thinking, picturing and imagining. When we choose to ask and to picture according to the Word, we allow that miracle power of the Holy Spirit to go forth from us to build a successful future.

All things are possible when agreement is made with God, regardless of the present situation. A seed planted within the heart of man produces after its kind. What seems impossible becomes possible.

*Jesus looked at them and said, "With man this is impossible, but not with God; all things are possible with God." (Mark 10: 27)*

What does "making new pictures within us" mean? The Bible says we are surrounded with a shield of favor. Can you picture that in your mind? Do you see yourself surrounded by favor (Psalm 5:12)? The Bible says that if our ways please the Lord, He makes even our enemies to be at peace with us (Proverbs 16:7). Do you see your enemies at peace with you? The Bible says wealth and riches are in your house, and that He fills your treasures full. Do you see riches in your house and your treasures full?

Jesus said everything is possible for the one who believes. The manifestation of the Spirit is the Word happening in the natural. Almost everything that happens in our lives is the result of a faith vision. When we have made use unknowingly of picturing the future, we have believed for destruction by planning how we would resolve that imagined crises.

We can see the effect of the pictures of our mind by studying the Old Testament. The exodus of the Israelites pictures our redemption in Christ. Before they came out of Egypt, blood (a picture of the blood of the New Covenant) was placed on their doorposts. They entered through blood which was to create a new place of blessings and take them from poverty and slavery to "a land flowing with milk and honey." They left with all the wealth of the wicked, with no sickness and disease, and with peace and joy in their hearts.

However, when Pharaoh and the Egyptians chased them, the Israelites remembered that they were slaves, beaten down, valueless, and impoverished. The Israelites were terrified.

> *They said to Moses, "Was it because there were no graves in Egypt that you brought us to the desert to die? What have you done to us by bringing us out of Egypt? Didn't we say to you in Egypt, 'Leave us alone; let us serve the Egyptians'? It would have been better for us to serve the Egyptians than to die in the desert!"*
> (Exodus 14:11-12)

The Egyptians represent the world or the devil pursuing the Christian. Just as the Israelites still viewed themselves as slaves, so also do Christians picture themselves being under circumstances instead of seeing themselves as conquerors. Thereafter, as Moses led them into the Promised Land, the Israelites accused Moses. The Israelites were in agreement with the devil, who is the accuser, because they continued to picture the lack and destruction they experienced as slaves in Egypt.

Even though the Israelites didn't die in the desert and God constantly performed one miracle after another, the Israelites remained connected to their experiences in slavery rather than receiving a new image of their future from God. The Israelites failed to meditate on the Promised Land.

As we discussed in the last chapter, ten of twelve spies sent by Moses to preview the Promised Land brought back a negative report (Numbers 13:27-33). They did not agree with God's plan for abundance; instead, they feared giants. They said they saw strong people and fortified cities, and that they saw themselves as grasshoppers.

The Israelites were reliving Egypt. Similarly, Christians who do not change their inner vision of others, of situations, and of themselves, continue in the cycle of failure they were experiencing before salvation. The Israelites saw themselves as grasshoppers, because grasshoppers are food for snakes (worshipped in Egypt) and because Egypt fed off Israelite slavery for hundreds of years.

**Our Destiny in the Word of God**

All Christians come out of the world into God's kingdom, bringing with them their own visions which rule them and determine their destiny. The Christian's destiny is set by the Word which God has written. Believing in destruction and disaster and in how we would handle it sets us up for failure. We see ourselves as food for the snake when we are in the world. We need to redecorate our inner house, and remove pictures of famine and destruction, and replace them with images from the Word of God. If we are connected to the Word and his supernatural miracles, disaster will not destroy us, because we will not come into agreement with that destruction in the same way that the Israelites did when they agreed with their enemy.

> God wrote His Word; we write down His promise.

God's promises are manifested in our lives by His binding Himself to His Word, by His resting on His Word (Hebrews 4:10), and by our agreeing with His Word. We receive His thoughts and are then in covenant with the cross. We are made in the likeness and image of God; we are meant to talk His talk, walk His walk, and think His thoughts. God wrote His Word; we write down His promise.

One time, God told me to write down all the blessing Scriptures, record my voice reading them onto a tape, and to then play my voice reading (and agreeing!) with the Scriptures all night on a recorder with an auto-reverse. It takes about two weeks to get used to. I have done this for twenty years, and I have discovered that the Scripture comes right into the subconscious. Jesus says:

> *And I will do whatever you ask in my name, so that the Son may bring glory to the Father. You may ask me for anything in my name, and I will do it.* (John 14:13-14)

> *If you remain in me and my words remain in you, ask whatever you wish, and it will be given you.* (John 15:7)

> *In that day you will no longer ask me anything. I tell you the truth, my Father will give you whatever you ask in my name. Until now you have not asked for anything in my name. Ask and you will receive, and your joy will be complete.* (John 16:23-24)

God has invited us into full partnership with Him. We are His proxies with power of attorney to do His will through agreement with His Word. We are His deputies to enforce the divine will and plan of God. We have been given His authority to implement His Word in the affairs of this earth. We are called to operate solely within the framework and system of God's Word. God will do nothing in the realm of this earth outside of that which agrees with His Word.

Made in God's image, we create with Him through faith visions. Deception says that God is responsible for what happens to us. Consider Adam's response as he was confronted by God.

> *The man said, "The woman you put here with me—she gave me some fruit from the tree, and I ate it."* (Genesis 3:12)

The man also was deceived and he blamed God for Eve's error. The truth is that we are co-creators with Jesus. As human beings, we must bear responsibility for what we create in our lives through thinking, speaking, seeing, writing, and doing. Faith pictures come from our thoughts,

> As human beings, we must bear responsibility for what we create in our lives.

so we can tap into our thoughts, take on the mind of Christ, and visualize in agreement with God's Word.

Most important of all, we must understand that what we do is preceded by what we see ourselves doing. We think first in order to form a picture within, and then we do the work, much in the same way that an engineer works. After all, building the first piano started with a thought, then a faith vision. Next, it was given a name and spoken into existence. Someone drew a sketch of it, wrote down the name, and labeled the parts. Thus, the first piano was built according to the vision.

A faith picture will excite you; then desire will begin and create the planning for doing it all.

## 7
### *Understanding Your Present State*

*The Lord will make you the head, not the tail.*
(Deuteronomy 28:13)

We are the heirs of Almighty God, and we have his exact intelligence. We are the head; we contain the mind and the intelligence of Christ. This is why the Word says, "I can do everything through him who gives me strength" (Philippians 4:13).

We have the mind of Christ when we agree with God's Word. When we agree with God, we enter into His intelligence. As we meditate the Word of God, His thoughts flow through our minds, empowering us to do His will. For us to think as God thinks, we must first understand our present state.

> *Then he opened their understanding, that they might understand the scriptures.* (Luke 24:45, KJV)

> *The eyes of your understanding being enlightened; that ye may know what is the hope of his calling, and what the riches of the glory of his inheritance in the saints.* (Ephesians 1:18, KJV)

*For this cause we also, since the day we heard it, do not cease to pray for you, and to desire that ye might be filled with the knowledge of his will in all wisdom and spiritual understanding.* (Colossians 1:9, KJV)

*And the spirit of the LORD shall rest upon him, the spirit of wisdom and understanding, the spirit of counsel and might, the spirit of knowledge and of the fear of the LORD; And shall make him of quick understanding in the fear of the LORD: and he shall not judge after the sight of his eyes, neither reprove after the hearing of his ears.* (Isaiah 11:2-3, KJV)

*Therefore do not be foolish, but understand what the Lord's will is.* (Ephesians 5:17)

Ephesians 1:18 refers to the eye of faith. Colossians 1:9 indicates that we should desire to be full of His will. Just one person can change this world for Christ. Moses and Abraham did. Daniel did, and you can, because God does not pick favorites; He is no respecter of persons. God says that in all wisdom and understanding, we need to have the eyes to see what the Spirit is showing us (Proverbs 2:2, 9, 11).

Our bank accounts, health, social lives, and positions at work reveal our present state. The physical manifestation of all our thinking, speaking, goal setting, planning, prioritizing, attitudes, focus, procrastination, and laziness result in our present condition.

Though the intellect can determine the meaning of external information, we still need to determine the direction of the Holy Spirit. When Tom and I learned that a world famous multi-millionaire, who has an international ministry, was coming to our church, we prayed diligently that we would connect to everything that God intended for us to grasp. We prayed that we would receive all that we needed, and after our anointed speaker had gone, we knew we were changed. The Holy Spirit aroused our attention and showed us things that anointed messengers talked about and told us to receive.

> It is important in the kingdom of God that we do what needs to be done and not waste time.

One aspect of change occurred when I began, supernaturally, to prioritize tasks in order by the Holy Spirit. It is important in the kingdom of God that we do what needs to be done and not waste time in the shuffle of urgent, but unimportant matters. God set goals; we see these goals throughout the Word. Thus, the Holy Spirit can keep us alert and can convict us of allowing our thoughts to become less than what God calls them to be.

The next week, I implemented the God-given ability to prioritize and set goals. I find the best time of day for high-priority items, and during that time, I let the answering service take care of the phone calls.

Focus, another important issue, opposes procrastination as an indicator of our present spiritual
state. Focus implies that we do not allow ourselves to
scatter our energy over a hundred different projects.
Such scattered energy rarely produces success.

Procrastination—the true failure—is actually
rooted in a fear of failure. Procrastination says, "Do
it tomorrow." Every time we think "Do it tomorrow,"
we can break that cycle of failure by doing it today!

## Be Alert

*Be self-controlled and alert. Your enemy the
devil prowls around like a roaring lion looking
for someone to devour.* (1 Peter 5:8)

When we see the life of Christ in the gospels,
we notice that He is constantly aware of the activity
around Him. Jesus was never caught by surprise
(Matthew 16:23; Mark 13:33-37).

*And pray in the Spirit on all occasions with all
kinds of prayers and requests. With this in mind,
be alert and always keep on praying for all the
saints.* (Ephesians 6:18)

*So then, let us not be like others, who are
asleep, but let us be alert and self-controlled.*
(1 Thessalonians 5:6)

Being alert, we cannot live in denial of current circumstances or attitudes. Denial is the counterfeit of true faith. We cannot change our present state by pretending that we are successful in every area if we are not driving out the thief. If the thief comes into our house and steals our furniture, VCR, and TV, we will not just sit around pretending he isn't there, because that would be denial. Instead, we face the fact of our present condition and use faith to fight for what is rightfully ours. We command the thief out by resisting him, which means to fight him with the Word of God.

Admitting our present state, we must continue to let the Holy Spirit examine us.

> *Examine yourselves to see whether you are in the faith; test yourselves. Do you not realize that Christ Jesus is in you—unless, of course, you fail the test?* (2 Corinthians 13:5)

If you sincerely wish to improve your present state and bring it into agreement with God's Word, you must deal with your present state at the cross (Chapter 8) and change your thoughts, images, and speech. Only the work of Christ at the cross can alter your future.

> *For though we live in the world, we do not wage war as the world does. The weapons we fight with are not the weapons of the world. On the contrary,*

*they have divine power to demolish strongholds.*
*We demolish arguments and every pretension that*
*sets itself up against the knowledge of God, and we*
*take captive every thought to make it obedient to*
*Christ.* (2 Corinthians 10:3-5)

**Future Crop**

Our speech reflects the images in our hearts,
and whatever we say sows our future crop (Galatians
6:7-8; Ephesians 4:30).

*Do not conform any longer to the pattern of this*
*world, but be transformed by the renewing of*
*your mind. Then you will be able to test and*
*approve what God's will is—his good, pleasing*
*and perfect will.* (Romans 12:2)

This creative transformation includes the
God-given principles of our being. God works with
individuals to produce a change through the process
of meditation.

*...you have taken off your old self with its prac-*
*tices and have put on the new self, which is*
*being renewed in knowledge in the image of its*
*Creator.* (Colossians 3:9-10)

God has given us, through the power of medita-
tion, the ability to take off the old self with its practices,

and build His will into our character and into the lives of others. If we ignore the work of the cross and fail to apply biblical principles, such as meditation, our lives will be the same in twenty years.

In the beginning, God told man to take dominion over the whole earth and to bring everything under subjection to God.

> *Therefore we do not lose heart. Though outwardly we are wasting away, yet inwardly we are being renewed day by day.* (2 Corinthians 4:16)

As we are inwardly renewed through the application of God's Word, we regain that dominion which we lost to the enemy. We have the ability and the right to take dominion, because we were born again with God's inheritance to build His kingdom into our lives.

> *For we are God's workmanship, created in Christ Jesus to do good works, which God prepared in advance for us to do.* (Ephesians 2:10)

God intends for us to experience abundance regardless of life's circumstances.

> *We went through fire and water, but you brought us to a place of abundance.*
> (Psalm 66:12)

Jesus taught a parable in which the enemy is pictured stealing the freshly sown Word. When you receive the Word of God, the enemy will come to persecute that Word within you. Will you let him steal it from you, or will you laugh at the enemy and shout, "I've already won!"?

The human spirit contains the abundance of the Almighty. The abundance is drawn out of us as we come into agreement with the Word by choosing appropriate thoughts, pictures, and words. We must no longer allow life's situations to dictate our thinking.

Even though we play scriptures all night long and awake with a prayer on our lips, a mere disappointing phone call or perhaps a small burden (if we allow it) comes to kill the Word. Worries are like weeds that try to choke out the root of godly thoughts and words. Worries are sins that must be hated as any sin is hated. The power of worry, frustration, and defeat must be broken so that we do not continually relive the process.

*Those who live according to the sinful nature have their minds set on what that nature desires; but those who live in accordance with the Spirit have their minds set on what the Spirit desires.* (Romans 8:5)

We must stop permitting our everyday life circumstances to control our thinking.

**Envy, Not Good**

God also says we are not to compare ourselves with one another, which causes envy.

> *But if you harbor bitter envy and selfish ambition in your hearts, do not boast about it or deny the truth. Such "wisdom" does not come down from heaven but is earthly, unspiritual, of the devil. For where you have envy and selfish ambition, there you find disorder and every evil practice.* (James 3:14-16)

Envy is pure foolishness. Another person's accomplishments result from their obedience to agreement with God—walking by faith. We do not need to envy anyone; we need only to change. Usually envy comes from a heart desire to want what we do not have. God says He will give us the desire of our hearts, and we cannot figure out in our intellect how that can be. Again, we try to resolve the situation in our own intellect, and such preoccupation is earthly, unspiritual wisdom, spawned by the enemy of our soul.

# 8
## Reject and Replace

One day, as I was meditating on His promises of healing in the Bible, the Holy Spirit spoke to me and said, "Maureen, there is an easier way. You have been going right to the resurrection and receiving the Word, but the power of the resurrection came through the cross, why do you avoid the cross? You need to go to the cross with the Holy Spirit and renew your mind. Remember that you have died with Christ to the curse and acknowledged God's plan. You now stand in His works and in all freedom from sin. At the cross, you receive Christ's humility by the renewing of your mind. See what He did for you and see Christ's total submission to God. Let the Holy Spirit show you how to fellowship with Christ suffering as He became your sin."

> *I want to know Christ and the power of his resurrection and the fellowship of sharing in his sufferings, becoming like him in his death, and so, somehow, to attain to the resurrection from the dead.* (Philippians 3:10-11)

You need to spend some time appreciating Christ Jesus for paying your sin in full. He took all the pain, suffering and heartache for you to totally set you free from the curse by becoming a curse for you. Then, faith in Christ's works would take root, and it would be evident that you hung with Him on the cross and your old man died there with all the generational curses and acts of the sinful nature. You could then enter into faith that you were redeemed for the blessing of Abraham.

> *Christ redeemed us from the curse of the law by becoming a curse for us, for it is written: "Cursed is everyone who is hung on a tree." He redeemed us in order that the blessing given to Abraham might come to the Gentiles through Christ Jesus, so that by faith we might receive the promise of the Spirit.* (Galatians 3:13-14)

Looking at the Serpent on the Pole

> *The LORD said to Moses, "Make a snake and put it up on a pole; anyone who is bitten can look at it and live." So Moses made a bronze snake and put it up on a pole. Then when anyone was bitten by a snake and looked at the bronze snake, he lived.* (Numbers 21:8-9)

*Just as Moses lifted up the snake in the desert, so the Son of Man must be lifted up...* (John 3:14)

*But I, when I am lifted up from the earth, will draw all men to myself.* (John 12:32)

*So Jesus said, "When you have lifted up the Son of Man, then you will know that I am the one I claim to be and that I do nothing on my own but speak just what the Father has taught me."* (John 8:28)

Jesus took on our sin at the cross and He became our substitute. The Israelites who looked upon the snake on the pole in the desert were healed and delivered from the curse so they could enter into the blessings of God. We need to visualize sin nailed to the cross and defeated there and see it becoming powerless and neutralized. We will then experience the power of God that has already delivered us in His eyes.

*When you were dead in your sins and in the uncircumcision of your sinful nature, God made you alive with Christ. He forgave us all our sins, having canceled the written code, with its regulations, that was against us and that stood opposed to us; he took it away, nailing it to the cross.* (Colossians 2:13-14)

Thereupon, you would come out of the curse and you would see that power of the enemy broken off your life. You would see yourself being able to receive the blessings.

**Death to the Chaff**

Jesus, speaking of Himself said:

> *I tell you the truth, unless a kernal of wheat falls to the ground and dies, it remains only a single seed. But if it dies, it produces many seeds.* (John 12:24)

The sin of the world becomes the chaff around the seed. Although Jesus did not sin, He took on the sins of the world and it became the chaff around Him. When the Word (the seed of God) battles with the sin of the flesh (chaff) within us, we must go to the cross and experience the death of that sin (chaff).

If, instead, you try to work the Word of God into your heart without removing the sin, then the sin persecutes the Word—a real war goes on inside of you.

> *For the sinful nature desires what is contrary to the Spirit, and the Spirit what is contrary to the sinful nature. They are in conflict with each other, so that you do not do what you want.* (Galatians 5:17)

*At that time the son born in the ordinary way persecuted the son born by the power of the Spirit. It is the same now. But what does the Scripture say? "Get rid of the slave woman and her son, for the slave woman's son will never share in the inheritance with the free woman's son."* (Galatians 4:29-30)

Suddenly, oppression, unbelief, and depression start taking over because you didn't take off the sin that so easily entangles us.

*Therefore, since we are surrounded by such a great cloud of witnesses, let us throw off everything that hinders and the sin that so easily entangles, and let us run with perseverance the race marked out for us.* (Hebrews 12:1)

You need to go to the cross and see sin defeated, dead and powerless there; see it gone forever from your life.

*In a large house there are articles not only of gold and silver, but also of wood and clay; some are for noble purposes and some for ignoble. If a man cleanses himself from the latter, he will be an instrument for noble purposes, made holy, useful to the Master and prepared to do any good work.* (2 Timothy 2:20-21)

*May I never boast except in the cross of our Lord Jesus Christ, through which the world has been crucified to me, and I to the world.* (Galatians 6:14)

During the time I was waiting for the physical manifestation of healing in my life that I had already received in my heart, there were two instances in the two months that I did not renew my mind in the victory. I did not see the disease nailed to the cross and defeated, nor did I see myself doing all the things the doctor said I couldn't do. On those two days, I was doing great in the morning, but by the end of the day, I was overwhelmed with doubt and unbelief, and the force of darkness came in like a flood to bring me into agreement with the disease that in the natural was incurable. Consequently, I realized I had to renew my mind daily to the health that I had already received in prayer. We must keep our minds in faith.

*Do you not know that in a race all the runners run, but only one gets the prize? Run in such a way as to get the prize. Everyone who competes in the games goes into strict training. They do it to get a crown that will not last; but we do it to get a crown that will last forever. Therefore I do not run like a man running aimlessly; I do not fight like a man beating the air. No, I beat my body and make it my slave so that after I have*

*preached to others, I myself will not be disquali-
fied for the prize.* (1 Corinthians 9:24-27)

We have to bring our minds into subjection to
the Word of God. The power of the gospel, the death,
burial and resurrection is there for us, yet the enemy
distracts us from it.

*I am not ashamed of the gospel, because it is the
power of God for the salvation of everyone who
believes: first for the Jew, then for the Gentile.
For in the gospel a righteousness from God is
revealed, a righteousness that is by faith from
first to last, just as it is written: "The righteous
will live by faith."* (Romans 1:16-17)

*Now, brothers, I want to remind you of the gospel
I preached to you, which you received and on
which you have taken your stand... For what I
received I passed on to you as of first importance:
that Christ died for our sins according to the
Scriptures...* (1 Corinthians 15:1, 3)

He keeps us busy and causes us to forget how
much we need the works of Christ in our lives to live
by faith. Within two months, I was totally well and in
perfect health. The specialists didn't know what to do
with me, for they could find no rheumatoid arthritis in
my body. What a miracle!

**The Promise to Abraham**
**Became Visible After Circumcision**
**(Picture of Cutting Away the Sins of the Flesh)**

Just as Abraham faced the fact that he was too old to have children, we must also face the fact that we cannot gain God's promises on our own.

> *Therefore, the promise comes by faith, so that it may be by grace and may be guaranteed to all Abraham's offspring—not only to those who are of the law but also to those who are of the faith of Abraham. He is the father of us all.* (Romans 4:16)

> *Against all hope, Abraham in hope believed and so became the father of many nations, just as it had been said to him, "So shall your offspring be." Without weakening in his faith, he faced the fact that his body was as good as dead—since he was about a hundred years old—and that Sarah's womb was also dead. Yet he did not waver through unbelief regarding the promise of God, but was strengthened in his faith and gave glory to God, being fully persuaded that God had power to do what he had promised. This is why "it was credited to him as righteousness."* (Romans 4:18-22)

It wasn't until Abraham was circumcised (picture of cutting away the sin of flesh) that the promised child, Isaac, could be conceived in the natural.

*You are to undergo circumcision, and it will be the sign of the covenant between me and you.* (Genesis 17:11)

*Now the LORD was gracious to Sarah as he had said, and the LORD did for Sarah what he had promised. Sarah became pregnant and bore a son to Abraham in his old age, at the very time God had promised him.* (Genesis 21:1-2)

It's the same with us. It's not until the sin of the flesh is cut away that we can conceive the promise in the natural.

*In him you were also circumcised, in the putting off of the sinful nature, not with a circumcision done by the hands of men but with the circumcision done by Christ, having been buried with him in baptism and raised with him through your faith in the power of God, who raised him from the dead. When you were dead in your sins and in the uncircumcision of your sinful nature, God made you alive with Christ. He forgave us all our sins.* (Colossians 2:11-13)

If we do not go to the cross and see those behavioral sins nailed to it, then we are going to be controlled by the uncircumcised flesh (the sin of the flesh) and give power to the devil.

Outside of identity with the death of Christ on the cross, it is impossible for the believer to change himself. If we want to have the desires of the Spirit of God fully met, we must come and let the Holy Spirit walk us through the works of Christ. We must let the Holy Spirit be our comforter, counselor and encourager. Much revelation comes from worshipping Jesus because of His works and acknowledging Him for what He has done in reconciling us to God through the cross.

> *...and in this one body to reconcile both of them to God through the cross, by which he put to death their hostility.* (Ephesians 2:16)

**Land Given to You**
**(Picture of the New Covenant Life)**

The Book of Joshua, a picture of the church age, shows us the life of the new covenant, the land flowing with milk and honey, and that Jesus did a complete work.

> *For no matter how many promises God has made, they are "Yes" in Christ. And so through him the "Amen" is spoken by us to the glory of God.* (2 Corinthians 1:20)

When we believe the Word of God, we receive this Promised Land for ourselves. In the land that the Israelites entered, there were giants and enemies. God told the Israelites that they had to drive them all out. The giants are a picture of the sin, or the aspects that have to be driven out of our lives.

> Outside of identity with the death of Christ on the cross, it is impossible for the believer to change himself.

God had the Word and the plan for the Israelites to drive out the enemy. In the eighth chapter of Joshua, the Israelites hung the king of Ai on a tree and left him hanging until evening. Everyone was to look at the king hanging on the tree as a curse.

> *Christ redeemed us from the curse of the law by becoming a curse for us, for it is written: "Cursed is everyone who is hung on a tree."* (Galatians 3:13)

This was a picture for us to see the curses in our lives—all those things that are contrary to the promises of God—were put away at the cross. We're not to live in the lack of blessings anymore.

The king represents the sin ruling that area of their lives. As the sun sets, Joshua orders him to be taken down from the tree and throws his body down at the entrance of the city gate. This is a picture of the strongholds in our lives totally defeated. The similarities to the crucifixion are obvious. This is just one of the many times in the Book of Joshua where a king of a city was hung on a tree to be looked at for the day.

If we do not apply the works of Calvary to our lives and allow Him to invade and live in us, we will continue to encounter seemingly insurmountable problems in our daily lives.

> *But if you do not drive out the inhabitants of the land, those you allow to remain will become barbs in your eyes and thorns in your sides. They will give you trouble in the land where you will live.* (Numbers 33:55)

> *But if you turn away and ally yourselves with the survivors of these nations that remain among you and if you intermarry with them and associate with them, then you may be sure that the LORD your God will no longer drive out these nations before you. Instead, they will become snares and traps for you, whips on your backs and thorns in your eyes, until you perish from this good land, which the LORD your God has given you.* (Joshua 23:12-13)

If we come into agreement with the things that are contrary to God's Word or character, we are making covenant with it and allowing the sin to remain. If we try to make a heaven here on earth, inviting the Word in, but failing to drive the sin out, it will become a trouble to us, a snare trap for us, whips on our backs and thorns in our eyes. The battle will continue within us. Receive the Word of God and drive out the enemy.

> *For if you live according to [the dictates of] the flesh, you will surely die. But if through the power of the [Holy] Spirit you are [habitually] putting to death (making extinct, deadening) the [evil] deeds prompted by the body, you shall [really and genuinely] live forever.* (Romans 8:13, AMP)

### Receive His Works

The Bible says that we no longer live, but that Christ lives in us. My life is hidden in Christ. At the cross, the law died; therefore, I no longer try to accomplish my needs and blessings in my own strength. I died to pride of self and received his humility at the cross. The Bible says God gives grace to the humble and when I find His works, I find grace.

> *So, my brothers, you also died to the law through the body of Christ, that you might belong to another, to him who was raised from the dead, in order that we might bear fruit to God.* (Romans 7:4)

> *But he gives us more grace. That is why Scripture says:*

*"God opposes the proud
but gives grace to the humble."*
(James 4:6)

*I have been crucified with Christ and I no longer live, but Christ lives in me. The life I live in the body, I live by faith in the Son of God, who loved me and gave himself for me.* (Galatians 2:20)

God showed me that at the cross, we find His righteousness (His right behavior).  If we are in our own righteousness, we cannot receive His righteousness.

*Since they did not know the righteousness that comes from God and sought to establish their own, they did not submit to God's righteousness.* (Romans 10:3)

At the cross, I find His righteousness so that I can die to my righteousness, which is just filthy rags to God.  The Bible says that if I'm trying to obtain God by the law to get His promises and to live this life, then I am clearly under a curse.  The law will never produce faith.  In the new covenant, we are in a life of faith.

At the cross, we also face the fact that we cannot overcome sin alone.  We need Christ's crucifixion and resurrection.  We realize He has the power to do what

He said He did, and we surrender to that resurrection by receiving the promises as complete in us.

In this chapter, we see the purpose of the death on the cross, and we see ourselves brought into the resurrection by the power of the Spirit. We want to know Christ intimately. Paul tells us how in Philippians 3:10. We share with Him at the cross. We become like Him in his death and somehow obtain the resurrection from the dead. With Him, we experience His death, burial and resurrection.

In the thirty plus years that Tom and I have been married, both of us have applied the gospel to every area of our lives. We went right to the cross and saw the Holy Spirit put to death all the behaviors of the flesh, and there we found His righteousness. In 1 Peter, chapter 2 and chapter 3, we see the application of the gospel for the marriage; in Romans we see the application of the gospel for the individual; and in Ephesians, we see the application of the gospel for the church.

## 9
## Perseverance: The Way to Maturity

This last chapter is a teaching that helped me in a very difficult time of the church.

> *[Love] always protects, always trusts, always hopes, always perseveres. Love never fails.* (1 Corinthians 13:7-8)

> *For Christ's love compels us.* (2 Corinthians 5:14)

If you can see it and believe it, you can do it. Jesus tried to tell us this in the Gospels. He tried to convince us that we, too, are capable of what He was doing, and that we could go a step further—doing even greater things !

> *I tell you the truth, anyone who has faith in me will do what I have been doing. He will do even greater things than these, because I am going to the Father.* (John 14:12)

When our minds can think the truth of Jesus (the mind of Christ) and genuinely believe (trust in) these thoughts, then we can achieve "greater things" by the power of the Holy Spirit.

> *Believe me when I say that I am in the Father and the Father is in me; or at least believe on the evidence of the miracles themselves.* (John 14:11)

Remember, regardless of how tough things get, we must continue to hold the truth in our minds and declare the truth (James 1:2-4; Ephesians 6:16; 1 Timothy 6:12). We will run up against a series of circumstances that will, for a time, almost convince us that we are actually going backwards, but perseverance is the key.

> *May the Lord direct your hearts into God's love and Christ's perseverance.* (2 Thessalonians 3:5)

> *But we are not of those who shrink back and are destroyed, but of those who believe and are saved.* (Hebrews 10:39)

The perseverance of Christ is the life of the Holy Spirit. We need perseverance along with purpose. We must continue to hold before our eyes the faith vision of God's success that is planted in us by the Holy Spirit. Even a dog will not give up an old bone, until it sees a fresh steak.  So, it is important to picture success as a motive for perseverance.

We must also understand that whatever is happening to us is what is happening to prepare us to receive the good we desire.  You can choose to become a victim of circumstances.  Then you can focus on SELF—self-pity, self-defeat—or  you can choose to be a winner and endure to the end.  The flesh does not want to do the Word

> The flesh does not want to do the Word or to persevere.

or to persevere.  Instead, it prefers sympathy.  If you hold on to your life, you lose your life.  If you hold on to your life, you lose your friends.  If you lose your life, you gain your friends.  If you hold on to your life, you lose your children.  If you lose your life, you gain your children.  If we are crucified in Christ, the flesh no longer rules our bodies.

Consider the motive for perseverance in these passages of Scripture:

> *...because you know that the testing of your faith develops perseverance. Perseverance must finish its work so that you may be mature and complete, not lacking anything.* (James 1:3-4)

> *Not only so, but we also rejoice in our sufferings, because we know that suffering produces*

*perseverance; perseverance, character; and character, hope. And hope does not disappoint us, because God has poured out his love into our hearts by the Holy Spirit, whom he has given us.* (Romans 5:3-5)

*...we consider blessed those who have perse-vered. You have heard of Job's perseverance and have seen what the Lord finally brought about. The Lord is full of compassion and mercy.* (James 5:11)

As we read the Book of Job, we see that Job was trying to do well in his own works by buying protection through fear. If it had been successful, Job would have looked like he was his own savior. When Job finally believed that he needed a redeemer, everything began to change. Job endured his sufferings until he could realize he needed the work of God in place of his own righteousness that was powerful against the devil.

*For this very reason, make every effort to add to your faith goodness; and to goodness, knowledge; and to knowledge, self-control; and to self-control, perseverance; and to perseverance, godliness;... For if you possess these qualities in increasing measure, they will keep you from being ineffec-tive and unproductive.* (2 Peter 1:5-6, 8)

**Facing Difficulties**

Being ineffective and unproductive results from, among other characteristics, a lack of perseverance. On the other hand, being great and effective evolves from facing difficult challenges. Success is the ability to withstand pain—physical, emotional, or mental. If we must endure hardship from the enemy for a season, we may as well endure it happily. We may as well "crucify the flesh" and choose to face challenges with joy and confidence. No matter what the devil throws at us, we have to hold the truth in our minds and declare it.

Hard times are neither a sign of wrongdoing nor an indication of a lack of faith. Jesus illustrated this point in the "Parable of the Sower" (Mark 4).

> *Some people are like seed along the path, where the word is sown. As soon as they hear it, Satan comes and takes away the word that was sown in them. Others, like seed sown on rocky places,... But since they have no root, they last only a short time. When trouble or persecution comes because of the word, they quickly fall away.* (Mark 4:15-17)

We can handle hard times by being doers of the Word. By practicing the Word we speak, we grow to a higher level of ministry, rather than mediocrity. Our business ventures become greater, instead of merely getting by, and we become effectually great in God, not timidly disabled in the kingdom.

*That is why, for Christ's sake, I delight in weaknesses, in insults, in hardships, in persecutions, in difficulties. For when I am weak, then I am strong.* (2 Corinthians 12:10)

Winston Churchill believed he would win the war, and he said so. He believed that his purpose in being born and living in that time was to lead Great Britain to victory. Each of us has a destiny in God, a purpose for our hour of birth. For this purpose, God has given us everything we need and more than we need to accomplish our goal. Therefore, we seek greater challenges.

We see people who seem great in the kingdom of God, but we don't know the pain they endured to become what they are. They must have been willing to deny the flesh, to make the way, and to seek a higher calling and greater vision in God. Great Christians become great because of the challenges they take on. Anybody in the world can have higher calling and greater vision in God. Great Christians become great because of the challenges they take on. Anybody in the world can float a boat downstream; it takes determination to go against the current.

We must decide to live our destiny by taking the challenges, going against the status quo, and rising above the problems.

**Six Strategies to Employ in Hard Times**

First, do what you can.

> *Finally, be strong in the Lord and in his mighty power. Put on the full armor of God so that you can take your stand against the devil's schemes. For our struggle is not against flesh and blood, but against the rulers, against the authorities, against the powers of this dark world and against the spiritual forces of evil in the heavenly realms. Therefore put on the full armor of God, so that when the day of evil comes, you may be able to stand your ground, and after you have done everything, to stand.* (Ephesians 6:10-13)

Don't be paralyzed with fear that will destroy you, but look for God's opportunity where you are and embrace it.

Second, have a church to share with. We need the corporate anointing. We should not isolate ourselves, because it is dangerous to do and is a sure way of failure. We are to be planted in the household of the Lord, part of the Body of Christ, and knitted together in love.

Third, we are to keep our minds focused on the Word of God in general and on specific words from God spoken to us. We are to remain in peace.

*You will keep in perfect peace
    him whose mind is steadfast,
    because he trusts in you.*
                        (Isaiah 26:3)

We are to make our minds submit to the will of God. We take on Christ's mind which is actively building God's kingdom within us. We are able to keep our minds set on that rather than on lower concerns.

Fourth, we are to speak the Word of God to our difficulty, or mountain, and not speak about our mountains. We tell the mountain to obey. Death and life are in our tongues.

Fifth, realize nothing happens as quickly as we wish it would.

*We want each of you to show this same diligence to the very end, in order to make your hope sure. We do not want you to become lazy, but to imitate those who through faith and patience inherit what has been promised.* (Hebrews 6:11-12)

*So do not throw away your confidence; it will be richly rewarded. You need to persevere so that when you have done the will of God, you will receive what he has promised.* (Hebrews 10:35-36)

Our flesh wants success now or yesterday. The worst days are often before the victory. We need the perseverance of Christ to produce the strength to stand. When we look back, it will not seem to be as long a time to wait.

Finally, stay committed to your destiny; the destiny has not changed. Problems should not alter your course; circumstances should not change your direction. Thomas Edison once had a factory that exploded into flames. As he was watching it, he told his son to get his mother. Edison's reason was that the fire was quite outstanding and he knew she would not want to miss it. He had a positive attitude.

> Stay committed to your destiny; the destiny has not changed.

The next day he gave his employees a pep talk and nonchalantly fell asleep on a park bench. No worries.

Henry Ford was persecuted by people who told him the automobile would not work and frightened animals. Nonetheless, he continued to succeed. What separates people like Henry Ford and Thomas Edison from the rest of the people is their perseverance toward their destiny.

We must also build God's picture within and never waiver.

*"For I know the plans I have for you," declares the LORD, "plans to prosper you and not to harm you, plans to give you hope and a future." (Jeremiah 29:11)*